School-Based Behavioral Assessment

The Guilford Practical Intervention in the Schools Series

Kenneth W. Merrell, Series Editor

Books in this series address the complex academic, behavioral, and social–emotional needs of children and youth at risk. School-based practitioners are provided with practical, research-based, and readily applicable tools to support students and team successfully with teachers, families, and administrators. Each volume is designed to be used directly and frequently in planning and delivering educational and mental health services. Features include lay-flat binding to facilitate photocopying, step-by-step instructions for assessment and intervention, and helpful, timesaving reproducibles.

Recent Volumes

Resilient Classrooms: Creating Healthy Environments for Learning
Beth Doll, Steven Zucker, and Katherine Brehm

Helping Schoolchildren with Chronic Health Conditions: A Practical Guide
Daniel L. Clay

Interventions for Reading Problems: Designing and Evaluating Effective Strategies
Edward J. Daly III, Sandra Chafouleas, and Christopher H. Skinner

Safe and Healthy Schools: Practical Prevention Strategies
Jeffrey R. Sprague and Hill M. Walker

School-Based Crisis Intervention: Preparing All Personnel to Assist
Melissa Allen Heath and Dawn Sheen

Assessing Culturally and Linguistically Diverse Students: A Practical Guide
Robert L. Rhodes, Salvador Hector Ochoa, and Samuel O. Ortiz

Mental Health Medications for Children: A Primer
Ronald T. Brown, Laura Arnstein Carpenter, and Emily Simerly

Clinical Interviews for Children and Adolescents: Assessment to Intervention
Stephanie H. McConaughy

Response to Intervention: Principles and Strategies for Effective Practice
Rachel Brown-Chidsey and Mark W. Steege

The ABCs of CBM: A Practical Guide to Curriculum-Based Measurement
Michelle K. Hosp, John L. Hosp, and Kenneth W. Howell

Fostering Independent Learning: Practical Strategies to Promote Student Success
Virginia Smith Harvey and Louise A. Chickie-Wolfe

Helping Students Overcome Substance Abuse: Effective Practices for Prevention and Intervention
Jason J. Burrow-Sanchez and Leanne S. Hawken

School-Based Behavioral Assessment: Informing Intervention and Instruction
Sandra Chafouleas, T. Chris Riley-Tillman, and George Sugai

School-Based Behavioral Assessment

Informing Intervention and Instruction

SANDRA CHAFOULEAS
T. CHRIS RILEY-TILLMAN
GEORGE SUGAI

THE GUILFORD PRESS
New York   London

© 2007 The Guilford Press
A Division of Guilford Publications, Inc.
72 Spring Street, New York, NY 10012
www.guilford.com

Printed in Canada

This book is printed on acid-free paper.

Last digit is print number: 9 8 7 6 5 4

Library of Congress Cataloging-in-Publication Data

Chafouleas, Sandra.
    School-based behavioral assessment : informing intervention and instruction / Sandra Chafouleas, T. Chris Riley-Tillman, George Sugai.
        p. cm.—(Guilford practical intervention in the schools series)
    Includes bibliographical references and index.
    ISBN-10: 1-59385-494-3   ISBN-13: 978-1-59385-494-2 (pbk. : alk. paper)
    1. Behavioral assessment of children.   2. Children with disabilities—Education.   3. Learning disabled children—Education.   4. Educational psychology.   I. Riley-Tillman, T. Chris.
II. Sugai, George M., 1951–   III. Title.
    LB1124.C43 2007
    370.15′3—dc22
                                                                                    2007021430

To our children—
Maggie, Zoe, James, Luke, Kiyoshi, and Reiko

About the Authors

Sandra Chafouleas, PhD, is an associate professor in the school psychology program and a research scientist with the Center for Behavioral Education and Research in the Neag School of Education at the University of Connecticut. Dr. Chafouleas's primary research interests involve the formative assessment of social behavior and the application of evidence-based strategies in schools. She has authored over 50 articles, book chapters, and books, and serves as the project director and co-principal investigator on Project VIABLE, an Institute of Education Sciences-funded grant with goals to develop and evaluate procedures for direct behavior rating scales to effectively and efficiently monitor and evaluate student behavior in the classroom. Dr. Chafouleas currently serves as associate editor of *School Psychology Review* and as an editorial board member of *Psychology in the Schools*. Prior to becoming a university trainer, she worked as a school psychologist and school administrator in a variety of settings dealing with children with behavior disorders.

T. Chris Riley-Tillman, PhD, is an assistant professor at East Carolina University with expertise in academic and social behavior assessment, intervention, school consultation, and the development and validation of assessment and intervention methodologies that are both empirically supported and feasible. Related to these interests, he is currently a co-principal investigator on Project VIABLE. Dr. Riley-Tillman has authored over 40 refereed journal articles and book chapters and currently serves as the associate editor for *School Psychology Forum* and as a board member for both *School Psychology Review* and the *Journal of Educational and Psychological Consultation*.

George Sugai, PhD, is a professor and the Carole J. Neag Endowed Chair in Special Education in the Neag School of Education at the University of Connecticut. His expertise is in behavior analysis, classroom and behavior management, schoolwide discipline, function-based behavior support, positive behavior supports, and educating students with emotional and behavioral disorders. He conducts applied school and classroom research and works with schools to translate research into practice. Dr. Sugai has been a teacher in the public schools, a treatment director in a residential program, and a program administrator. He is currently co-director of the Center on Positive Behavioral Interventions and Supports at the University of Connecticut and the University of Oregon and director of the Center for Behavioral Education and Research in the Neag School of Education.

Acknowledgments

Although we have many people to acknowledge, we must start by expressing our most sincere appreciation to Amy Briesch for her tireless work in discussing ideas and helping us to pull the project together. We also are grateful to Teri LeBel for her editorial eye and Jim Wright for his constructive feedback and useful materials. Craig Thomas of The Guilford Press also must be acknowledged for his continuous and positive enthusiasm. Of course, we thank the many mentors and colleagues who have helped shape our thinking and practices over the years. Finally, we give our greatest thanks to our spouses (EJ, Erin, and Betsy) and families who provide unfaltering support and keep us connected to the real world.

Contents

1

Introduction to
School-Based Behavioral Assessment

The primary purpose of this book is to provide information about behavioral assessment methods and practices as they apply to school settings. Although a seemingly straightforward task, school-based behavioral assessment can take on different meanings depending on a number of contextual variables. Thus, an important first goal in this chapter is to establish our definition of school-based assessment as a guide for using this book. To begin, we draw your attention to our inclusion of "informing intervention and instruction" within the title. This addition expands a definition of assessment beyond a narrow view that implies an endpoint, or static nature, to the assessment process, such as is found in practices focused on diagnosis or classification. That is, our view is that school-based behavioral assessment encompasses practices that can continually inform decisions about instruction and intervention. Data gleaned from such assessment practices are needed in order to enable frequent evaluation of performance, which tells us when changes to instruction and intervention are warranted. Understanding progress toward goal attainment serves as the fundamental reason why we engage in assessment.

Once we accept this general definition of and rationale for school-based behavioral assessment, the next "big" consideration is to determine which assessment data are needed. To do this you need to understand (1) why you need the data, (2) what decisions will be made using these data, (3) which tools are best matched to assess the behavior of interest, and (4) what resources are available to collect these data. These questions are used throughout the book to guide decisions about assessment methods and practices. We expand on each later in this chapter, but first return to further exploration of definitions of and reasons for engaging in school-based behavioral assessment.

1

WHAT IS SCHOOL-BASED BEHAVIORAL ASSESSMENT AND WHY IS IT NEEDED?

Although required in some situations (e.g., special education identification, statewide initiatives), school-based behavioral assessment should be considered a process for using data to identify and solve a problem rather than a requirement. As noted by Merrell, Ervin, and Gimpel (2006), this model for using assessment data to solve a problem is outcome focused and context specific. That is, assessment becomes a process of collecting information for a specific reason (i.e., a problem) and with a specific use (i.e., to solve that problem). In schools, the "problem" typically relates to a difference between current and expected performance in some domain, and thus assessment data are used to determine why the discrepancy exists, which then informs directions for instruction and intervention. In turn, data continue to be collected in order to assess the effects of the change in instruction and intervention aimed at eliminating that discrepancy. Additionally, in our view, assessment needs to involve both *effective* and *efficient* data-based decision making. Although we certainly agree with training standards advocated by the National Association of School Psychologists, which has stated that "data-based decision-making permeates every aspect of professional practice" (2000, p. 15), we also acknowledge constraints in applied settings on collecting meaningful, high-quality data in an efficient manner. As the response-to-intervention (RTI) approach to determining student needs becomes more widely implemented, it will be a significant challenge to support educators in the use of efficient assessment procedures that allow effective data-based decision making in daily activities. Thus we define school-based behavioral assessment as involving an understanding of why it is being done and how the data will be used, and also acknowledging the need to direct attention toward efficient use of resources for collecting and using assessment data.

Given that this book is about school-based assessment, we focus on student academic and social behavior outcomes. This focus on students presents additional issues that must be considered when planning and conducting assessment with children. First, it is important to remember that children enter the educational system as a result of adult concern and responsibility (Mash & Wolfe, 1999). Given their minor and dependent status, children do not self-refer to attend school. Instead, they are required to attend school by community, parental, and school mandate. Second, assessment data typically do not come directly from the child, but instead from an adult (i.e., teacher, parent) who is familiar with the child. Thus, data may be biased to varying degrees based on adult perception of and experience with the child. In addition, these perceptions can vary across adults. Third, because students vary developmentally by age, grade, family, and so forth, assessment and monitoring also must be sensitive, flexible, and accurate. As noted by Mash and Wolfe (1999), a problem presented by a child can be transitory, minor, or severe in nature, depending on the child's developmental status, context, and learning history. For example, assessment data may indicate that a child has a bedwetting episode on average two times per week. Our analysis of these data will be dependent on whether the student is 4 or 16 years old!

Finally, as noted by Mash and Wolfe (1999), interventions for children are usually intended to promote further development rather than restore a previous level of functioning. Thus intervention planning for children should always emphasize inclusion of skills-based components. That is, children should be taught directly those skills that are needed to promote positive development. All of these considerations lend further support to an assessment model that uses data-based decision making to inform instruction and intervention. Adopting a problem-solving model of behavioral assessment then requires consideration as to where assessment efforts should be focused and which tools can best provide needed information.

HOW ARE DECISIONS MADE ABOUT WHERE TO FOCUS ASSESSMENT EFFORTS?

Traditionally, assessment has been considered from the individual perspective, for example, to determine special education eligibility. Such a narrow perspective neglects consideration of the context or environment in which the individual is functioning. Emphasis on the problem as solely within an individual can miss important contributing indicators within the school context. For example, when conducting assessments related to "attention difficulties," observational data taken only on a single student may be misleading. When examined in isolation, a student who is estimated to be "off-task" during 80% of observed intervals may be considered for a diagnosis of attention-deficit/hyperactivity disorder. However, this decision may be different if additional observations indicate that most students in the same context engage in "off-task" behavior during 75% of the intervals.

Thus, determining what question needs to be answered also includes consideration of where to focus assessment, for example, the individual student in a particular classroom or grade, or a group of students at the school or district level. A wider view of possible targets of assessment may allow us to engage in proactive or preventive efforts that serve more than a single individual—and even decrease the amount of individual assessment and intervention we have to do! The schoolwide positive behavior support (SWPBS) approach, which emphasizes the prevention of behavior problems by establishing a continuum of positive behavior support practices, provides a useful way to organize thinking about possible levels of assessment. Although detail with regard to the features that characterize SWPBS is provided in Chapter 2 (see also *www.pbis.org*), we review the continuum here to illustrate the need for a wider view of assessment targets.

The SWPBS continuum, taken from a public health prevention framework, is usually operationalized into three tiers (Walker et al., 1996): primary, secondary, and tertiary (see Figure 1.1). The primary, or universal, level encompasses efforts aimed at all staff and students in a school/classroom. Generally, about 80% of students will respond positively to this level of prevention, and will not need more intensive intervention efforts. At the primary level, prevention strategies are focused on creating environments that promote student learning and engagement, such as identifying common behavioral expectations and explicating teaching and supporting demonstration of these socially appropriate behaviors (Ervin, Schaughnency, Matthews, Goodman, & McGlinchey, 2007). An important contributor to the success of primary prevention is formative evaluation of the effectiveness of those activities—that is, assessment at the level of the whole school or class. As

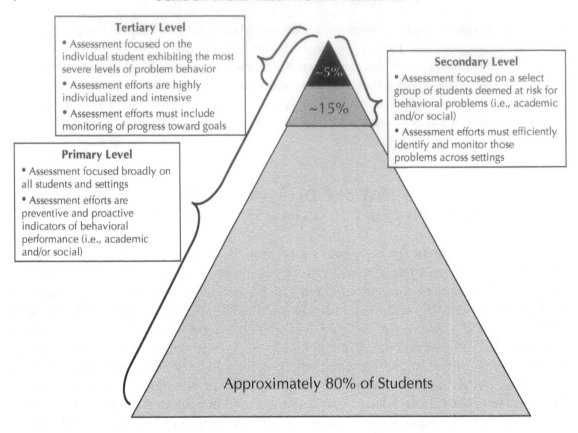

Tertiary Level
- Assessment focused on the individual student exhibiting the most severe levels of problem behavior
- Assessment efforts are highly individualized and intensive
- Assessment efforts must include monitoring of progress toward goals

Secondary Level
- Assessment focused on a select group of students deemed at risk for behavioral problems (i.e., academic and/or social)
- Assessment efforts must efficiently identify and monitor those problems across settings

Primary Level
- Assessment focused broadly on all students and settings
- Assessment efforts are preventive and proactive indicators of behavioral performance (i.e., academic and/or social)

~5%

~15%

Approximately 80% of Students

FIGURE 1.1. A continuum of assessment and intervention activities.

discussed in Chapter 2, assessment data that can be valuable at this level include existing schoolwide data such as office discipline referrals. For example, Mrs. Brown, the elementary principal, might call you into her office to share her frustration at the number of students being sent to her office during lunch periods. In fact, as you look around her office, you think to yourself that there seem to more second-grade students sprawled around the main office than actually eating their lunch in the cafeteria! So, you pull a summary of office discipline referrals over the past month and find that, indeed, second-grade students from Mr. Smith's class have had substantially more referrals than other groups of students. Thus you propose a plan that entails teaching the expectations for cafeteria behavior to Mr. Smith's students along with instituting better monitoring of those students in the cafeteria to support positive behavior and reduce inappropriate behavior. And in the end, you have saved the day in Mrs. Brown's eyes—without exerting significant assessment effort or developing multiple individualized intervention plans.

Secondary, or targeted, assessment and intervention are provided for students who display at-risk behavior and need more behavioral support than universal or primary prevention. It has been estimated that approximately 15% of students will fall within this level. Students may be first identified as at risk based on assessment data generated from the primary level. For example, in the cafeteria example above, perhaps your discipline referral data indicate that four students comprise 70% of the total number of cafeteria referrals following implementation of the intervention for Mr. Smith's class. Thus this group of students might serve as the target for secondary level prevention efforts. In this case, it might be appropriate to continue using office discipline referrals as an assessment tool. However, additional data might also be considered depending on the intervention strategy employed. For example, suppose that you develop a self-management intervention for these students with regard to cafeteria behavior, which is implemented by the cafeteria aide. The intervention involves daily rating of the degree to which expected cafeteria behaviors were displayed, using a scale from 1 (not displayed) to 5 (perfectly displayed). In this case, it could be useful to use the self-management data as another assessment tool because (1) the data already exist and thus resources are not burdened to collect them (it's efficient!) and (2) it may be more sensitive than discipline referrals in capturing behavior that is not severe enough to warrant an office referral yet may be on the path toward it (it's effective at telling us what is or is not working!). Thus using the existing rating data to identify areas (e.g., times, particular behavior) in need of further teaching and/or support can be considered efficient and effective data-based decision making. As noted by Ervin and colleagues (2007), localized data-driven problem solving that examines behavior in context is needed for effectiveness at the secondary and tertiary levels.

As with the secondary level, tertiary (or select) level assessment and intervention strategies are provided for students who are not responding to instruction and intervention at the primary and secondary levels. Approximately 5% of these students will need this type of highly individualized intervention. Given their high-risk status, assessment strategies are also likely to be highly individualized and may be used in functional behavior assessment. That is, although schoolwide data such as office discipline referrals may be helpful in providing a piece of a total assessment picture, additional information is likely to be needed as well. In this case, assessment tools capable of providing specific and detailed information regarding an individual's behavior, such as systematic direct observation or behavior rating scales, may be needed. For example, in the above cafeteria example, we may find that one of Mr. Smith's students continues to have difficulty following the secondary-level intervention. Further exploration of schoolwide data regarding this student suggests behavioral problems exist across multiple settings. So you may need to further investigate the reason for the behavioral problems—such as by having multiple adults complete a behavior rating scale and also conducting systematic direct observation in various settings. Those additional data, coupled with our existing schoolwide data and daily cafeteria behavior ratings, should lead us to better understanding of the reason for the problem behavior as well as potential interventions that are likely to work (i.e., are conceptually relevant). Thus tertiary-level assessment typically involves assessment focused on the individual student—and should also involve assessment that includes progress monitoring, given the likelihood of intensive intervention plan implementation and corresponding need to evaluate the effectiveness of that plan in a formative as well as summative fashion.

In summary, when engaging in assessment in schools, the level of assessment most appropriate for the presenting problem must be determined as well as which assessment tools best provide the information needed to solve the problem. Although the unit of analysis for data interpretation and the target for intervention vary, problem solving occurs at the individual student, classroom, and schoolwide levels (Ervin et al., 2007). As previously noted, efficient and effective data-based decision making involves good problem identification, which includes determining which and how much data are needed to solve the problem. However, for the data to be accurate and useful, the process by which the data are collected also must be effective and efficient. In the next section, we focus on various considerations to guide selection of particular assessment tools.

HOW ARE ASSESSMENT TOOLS SELECTED?

An overarching principle that guides how assessment tools are selected is to approach assessment from a multimethod, multisource, and multisetting perspective. In general, the more relevant the data that are available, the better our ability to answer specific assessment questions. For example, although a particular behavior may be most problematic in a school cafeteria, an intervention plan could be more effective if other individuals in other settings are also included. Thus, multiple assessment methods (e.g., direct observation, rating scales) are needed to collect data from multiple sources (e.g., teachers, parent, peers) across a variety of settings (e.g., cafeteria, hallways, restrooms). One limitation of this approach, however, is that more does not always mean easier or better. Collecting lots of information can be time consuming and cumbersome, and the quality of the data might therefore be affected. A balance must be achieved between collecting enough information to understand a problem situation and develop an intervention plan and ensuring high quality, accuracy, and relevance. For example, a teacher's daily homework record that is maintained in the classroom grade book may be more efficient and just as relevant as a daily written log that is completed by the student, parent, and teacher to duplicate recording of homework completion. In this example, some precision might be lost with regard to understanding the context in which homework is or is not being completed; however, feasibility may outweigh precision in this case. In summary, multimethod, multisetting, multisource assessment practices should be given priority; however, each assessment situation should be evaluated carefully to maintain precision in the context of quantity. To assist in achieving this balance, we now address the four guiding questions to consider when selecting assessment tools:

- Why do you need the data?
- Which tools are best matched to assess the behavior of interest?
- What decisions will be made using the data?
- What resources are available to collect the data?

Why Do You Need the Data?

Understanding the need for data requires a clear understanding of the purpose of the assessment. For example, if the intent is to identify students who are at risk with regard to a particular behavior (e.g., early literacy skills) or to provide an evaluative statement of the effects of an after-school program to enhance reading skills, desired level of assessment generalization (or in some cases specificity) might be considered (Riley-Tillman,

Kalberer, & Chafouleas, 2005). That is, is the purpose of the assessment to provide an aggregated statement about a child's behavior (generalization) or to determine information about a particular behavior at a particular time or in a specific setting (specificity or directness)? The reason you need the data drives the type of assessment (and then also the methods and practices used in the assessment). Generally, assessments are conducted for four main reasons: (1) evaluation, (2) screening, (3) diagnosis, and (4) progress monitoring.

Evaluation

Evaluative assessment provides a general summary of student skills, such as district- or state-mandated year-end testing. The results provide an indicator of the overall effectiveness of an intervention, whether global (e.g., reading curriculum for the entire second grade) or specific (4-month intensive social skills program for a student with autism). Evaluative assessment is used to confirm the implementation of a given practice rather than to inform day-to-day decisions about student performance and instruction. These summative tools must have established psychometric standards and provide consumer-relevant information.

Screening

The purpose of screening assessments is to identify students considered at risk for difficulty in a particular area (e.g., math, social skills) who would benefit from the addition of or change to an intervention. Generally, screening tools are administered to a population (e.g., all first-grade students) on a periodic basis (e.g., first of year, beginning of semester) to determine if current and expected levels of performance are discrepant. Significant discrepancies are often predictive of future problems or risks, and early interventions are usually indicated. In their discussion of good screening tools for use in early literacy assessment, Good, Simmons, and Kame'enui (2001) noted that screening tools must have predictive power and decision making utility. Predictive power is the ability to reliably and accurately identify those students likely to have difficulty in the future based on assessment information about the current level of performance. Screening tools are not intended to provide in-depth assessment information about a particular skill area, but only to indicate that a significant or important discrepancy is present.

Diagnosis

Diagnostic assessment provides in-depth information about student skills and needs. Rather than quick identification of a potential problem using a critical indicator, a comprehensive picture of student behavior is provided, including performance strengths and weaknesses. In their discussion of diagnostic assessment of academic behavior, Howell and Nolet (2000) describe how both survey and specific-level assessment may be used. For example, one might assess a student on many behaviors to determine which skills fall significantly below expected performance levels. An in-depth assessment of a select narrow range of behaviors typically follows to more clearly identify the areas in need of intervention. To be meaningful in schools, diagnostic assessments also must focus on the environment in which the behavior is (or is not) exhibited. This ecological information is critical in understanding the behavior as a functional response to a set of contingencies rather than something that exists in a vacuum. Settings must be evaluated because different environmental conditions affect the likelihood of behavioral events in different ways. Diagnostic assessment can be helpful in enhancing conceptually relevant intervention decisions, which refers to the selection of instructional strategies based on identified needs rather than a trial-and-error approach (see Erchul & Martens, 2002, for a discussion of conceptual relevance in school-based consultation).

Progress Monitoring

Progress monitoring refers to the collection of information on a frequent and repeated basis. These data are collected over time to determine if progress trends indicate that goals will or are being met. Collection of repeated information enables intervention decisions to be made early in the instructional or behavior change process rather than waiting until the end of a period (e.g., school year), when enhancements or changes may be less effective or efficient. The frequency of data collection for progress monitoring can vary widely (e.g., three times per year to three times per day). As with screening measures, these data provide general indicators of student performance. Given the frequent repeated administration, progress monitoring measures need to be administered efficiently and constructed in multiple forms. Although summative assessment practices play an important role when identifying a problem and evaluating intervention effectiveness, the addition of ongoing feedback on student performance through progress monitoring over the short and long term deserves special consideration. For example, rather than discovering 3 months after implementing a time-intensive program to teach positive playground skills (summative assessment) that it was actually not working after the first 3 weeks of implementation, frequent and regular monitoring of an indicator of positive skill (such as the absence of verbal and physical altercations) would suggest a change in the use of the program much earlier. As noted by Howell and Nolet (2000), "the more frequent the assessment, the more often one can make data-based decisions" (p. 188). Given limited resources and time, schools cannot afford to waste days, months, or years on ineffective methods.

As previously discussed, understanding the purpose of the assessment also includes examining the level at which it should be focused. In some situations, assessment of the individual student may be appropriate. In other contexts, classroom- or schoolwide assessment questions would be more appropriate. For example, although a student may have been referred because of displays of aggressive behavior, extended assessments determine that other students in that classroom also exhibit similar behavior. With this additional information, a group-based contingency plan would be developed rather than an individualized behavior support plan as initially assumed. Armed with an understanding of why data are needed, and at which level data should be collected, it is time to move on to the remaining guiding questions.

Which Tools Are Best Matched to Assess the Behavior of Interest?

Selected assessment tools should provide relevant information regarding the target behavior(s), contexts in which those behaviors are observed, and distal events that, although not immediate, affect the occurrence of the target behaviors in the problem context. For example, selecting attendance data does not help inform intervention decisions related to increasing proactive skills on the playground. Riley-Tillman and colleagues (2005) have referred to the match of assessment tool to the behavior and context as "goodness of fit." Not all assessment tools adequately measure the same behaviors (McDougal, Chafouleas, & Waterman, 2006). As an example, behavior rating scales that assess a student's general state or status relative to a wide range of behaviors would not be useful when rating "out of seat" behavior events per hour during math instruction. Similarly, within a class of tools such as direct observation, a good fit between what behavior is measured and how must be considered. For example, a direct observation duration recording method (i.e., what percent of class time did the student spend out of seat?) would yield different outcome data than an event recording method (e.g., how many times during a class period was the student out of seat?).

What Decisions Will Be Made Using These Data?

Determining the type of decision to be made helps guide what assessment tools are selected. High-stakes decisions (e.g., curriculum adoption) or individualized behavior support planning requires data in whose accuracy and relevance users have a high degree of confidence. Confidence is related to the degree of inference needed when interpreting the data. One indicator for determining directness is the extent to which the collected information is removed in time and place from the actual occurrence of the behavior (see Cone, 1978). For example, behavior rating scales are considered indirect because the information is collected from another person, who responds to items based on his or her perception of the student's behavior. In contrast, direct observation is considered direct in that the assessments occur as the behaviors are observed. As a general rule of thumb, "high-stakes cases" (e.g., serious disruption or potential harm to the student or others, consideration of change to a more restrictive setting) should include direct assessment tools. In general, the more direct the measure, the more resource intensive the data collection (i.e., feasibility).

What Resources Are Available to Collect These Data?

Determining the resources required to collect data is equally important when selecting assessment tools (i.e., how feasible is it to collect the data in a given situation?). Feasibility refers to consideration, for example, of time needed to train a person to accurately use the tool, intrusiveness of using the tool in the required setting, time and scheduling for data collection, complexity of using the tool, and so forth. For example, asking a teacher to monitor student behavior each day, all day, and for a full semester may not be possible given class size, training needs, assessment fluency, and other instructional responsibilities. Feasibility also is related to considering the costs versus the benefits associated with summative versus frequent progress monitoring.

CONCLUDING COMMENTS

The goal of this chapter was to consider the importance of assessment in decision making. A critical recurring theme is that assessments should be planned and purposeful, which means having clear, measurable, and multiple questions from the outset of the assessment process. Those questions involve understanding (1) why data are needed and (2) which data are needed. When questions are specified in measurable terms, more efficient and effective data-based decision making is possible. In the next chapter, we consider level of assessment with a chapter dedicated to assessment at the whole-school level (primary). The following four chapters are dedicated to review of specific assessment tools that you may likely choose when engaged in more individualized and specialized assessments and interventions (see Table 1.1). Within each of those chapters, guidelines are presented for evaluating each tool in the context of the questions that are being addressed. In Chapter 7, additional guidelines are discussed to enhance selection and use of assessment tools and decision making. Finally, procedures for summarizing and interpreting data are described in the Appendix at the end of the book.

TABLE 1.1. Types of School-Based Behavioral Assessment Tools Reviewed in This Book

Tool	Chapter reviewed
Whole-school data	2
Extant data	3
Systematic direct observation	4
Direct behavior ratings	5
Behavior rating scales	6

2

Behavioral Assessment within the Context of the Whole School

Schools are busy organizations that have the important mission of preparing children and youth to be successful members of society. The job is complex because students, staff, and families differ in many ways (e.g., learning histories, cultural backgrounds, home practices, economic resources, and status). To maximize success for each and every student, schools must be effective, efficient, and relevant in how they organize and utilize resources and activities, especially in relation to establishing and maintaining positive and safe school climates (Colvin, Kame'enui, & Sugai, 1993; White, Algozzine, Audette, Marr, & Ellis, 2001). One of our most important strategies for accomplishing this goal is to use whole-school information or data to guide schoolwide decisions relative to what, how, where, and when something is done.

In this chapter, we focus on the use of behavior-related data to make decisions for improving the social climates and teaching environments of classroom and non-classroom settings for all students and staff. We begin by describing the characteristics of a positive whole-school context, with an emphasis on the role of assessment. Next, we discuss how effective and efficient data-based decision making may start with use of existing data sources, such as office discipline referrals, at the whole-school level. Finally, we review strengths and weaknesses of using office discipline referrals in school-based behavioral assessment.

WHY LOOK AT THE WHOLE-SCHOOL CONTEXT?

To support teaching and maximize achievement, schools must maintain learning environments that foster effective self-management, promote supportive and proactive social relations, and maximize academic and instructional engagement. A proactive learning environment also helps prevent the development of antisocial aggressive behavior

(Dwyer, Osher, & Hoffman, 2000; Gottfredson, Gottfredson, & Hybl, 1993; Morrison & Skiba, 2001), overuse of reactive punishment consequences (Skiba & Peterson, 1999, 2000; Skiba, Peterson, & Williams, 1997), dropping out of school (Bowditch, 1993), and disproportionate and inappropriate use of suspension and expulsion with students from racially diverse backgrounds (McFadden, Marsh, Price, & Hwang, 1992; Skiba et al., 1997; Townsend, 2000) or special education contexts (Morrison & D'Incau, 2000; Rose, 1988).

Achieving a safe, productive, respectful, and protective learning and teaching environment is related to how well the school functions and supports all students and staff members (Mayer & Leone, 1999). The whole-school context encompasses all students and all staff members across all school settings (Colvin et al., 1993).

In recent years, the practices and systems of effective whole school efforts, also referred to as schoolwide positive behavior support systems (SWPBS), have been identified and demonstrated (Horner & Sugai, 2005; Safran & Oswald, 2003; Sugai & Horner, 2002). Six major features characterize SWPBS: (1) lead with a team, (2) adopt a systems perspective, (3) teach and encourage prosocial skills, (4) discourage rule-violating behaviors, (5) maintain a continuum of positive behavior support for all students, and (6) use data to guide decision making and action planning (McCurdy, Mannella, & Eldridge, 2003; McEvoy & Walker, 2000; Metzler, Biglan, Rusby, & Sprague, 2001; Sugai, Horner, et al., 2000). Brief descriptions of these SWPBS characteristics follow.

Leading with a Team

Although many schools introduce new practices and initiatives through whole-school meetings and inservice events, the adoption of these practices is often incomplete and not sustained. Effective schools establish leadership teams that lead the adoption and sustained implementation of effective practices by (1) ensuring adequate representation from and participation by the school (e.g., teachers, specialists, nonteaching staff, family members, students, community members), (2) ensuring administrator participation, (3) using data to contextualize implementation of school practices, (4) establishing formal leadership standing, and (5) communicating effectively among themselves and their school colleagues. Successful teams use their schoolwide behavioral data to identify what they would like to improve or change, what they need to do to make those improvements, and whether they are successful in achieving those changes.

Adopting a Systems Perspective

With so many initiatives and activities being implemented in schools, efficient schools adopt a systems perspective to improve the characteristics and functioning of the whole school (Sugai, Horner, et al., 2000). As displayed in Figure 2.1, from a SWPBS perspective four intertwined elements must be considered (Sugai & Horner, 2002). First, schools must identify measurable, achievable, and contextually relevant *outcomes*, both academic and related to social behavior. These outcomes guide schools so they know where they are headed, whether they are getting there, and what changes need to be made to improve their efforts. Second, schools must use local *data* to specify measurable out-

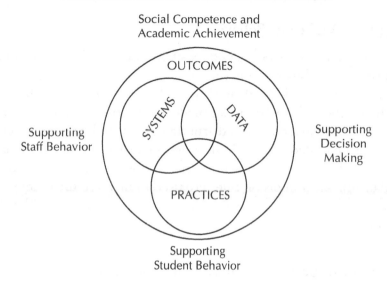

FIGURE 2.1. Four elements of SWPBS.

comes, select practices that are likely to lead to those outcomes, and assess progress toward achieving those outcomes. Third, schools must select *practices* that have sound evidence supporting the achievement of student and school-specified outcomes. Finally, schools must have *systems* (e.g., team, data, ongoing professional development, local coaching/facilitation) in place to give school personnel the capacity to implement practices accurately, efficiently, and effectively and achieve maximum outcomes.

Although the emphasis in this book is on collection and use of data, it is important to understand the role that each of the four factors plays. The overlapping relationship of outcomes, data, practices, and systems is designed to increase the relevance and quality of implementation efforts and outcomes. For example, schools that pay attention to all four elements avoid adopting practices that are not aligned with the data-verified needs of the school, are not scientifically supported with sound research, or are not implemented with accuracy or durability because staff members have not been trained adequately.

Teaching and Encouraging Prosocial Skills

SWPBS gives priority to the identification of a small number of schoolwide expectations (three to five) that are positively stated (e.g., "be respectful"), defined with observable behavioral examples (e.g., "Being responsible is having school materials to complete class work"), and taught in the context in which they are needed (e.g., "Being safe is crossing the street to the school at the corner crosswalk") (Lewis & Sugai, 1999; Taylor-Greene et al., 1997). When these expectations are taught well, students incorporate the expectations into their language and communications, school personnel give students corrective and encouraging feedback based on these expectations, and occurrences of prosocial behavior are more likely than problem behaviors. The goal is to deemphasize punishment-oriented disciplinary practices and polices that actually may promote the development and occurrence of problem behavior (Hyman & Perone, 1998; Reinke & Herman, 2002).

Discouraging Rule-Violating Behaviors

Effective schools focus on encouraging positive schoolwide expectations. However, SWPBS schools also establish a continuum of consequences for rule-violating behavior. Problem behaviors are defined in observable and mutually exclusive terms (nonoverlapping). In addition, distinctions are made among rule violations at three basic levels: (1) minor (teacher managed—e.g., disrupting other students, late to class); (2) major (office/administrator handled—e.g., physical fighting, repeated insubordination/noncompliance); and (3) district (board/community involvement—e.g., illegal drug possession, weapons, vandalism). Clear decision rules are used to increase the efficiency of interventions (e.g., three repeated minors = major, third major is associated with referral to counselor or behavioral support team).

Maintaining a Continuum of Positive Behavior Supports

SWPBS schools emphasize prevention of problem behaviors by establishing a continuum of positive behavior support practices. This continuum is usually operationalized into three tiers (Walker et al., 1996). Primary, or universal tier, intervention strategies are intended to prevent the development and occurrence of rule violating behaviors by promoting the teaching and encouragement of prosocial behaviors for all students by all staff across all school settings. For example, when the staff of Lakeview Elementary School decided to implement SWPBS, they voted to establish three school rules: be respectful, be responsible, and be safe. They decided that these rules would be taught to all students on the first day of the school year, both in the classroom and in nonclassroom settings. To reinforce students for desirable behavior, the SWPBS team created "behavior bucks," which students could earn for following the school rules and then enter into a drawing for small prizes from the school store. This program targeted all students in the school and was therefore considered to be a primary level intervention. To effectively manage and monitor behavioral data for the entire school, the administrative team chose to collect and summarize office discipline referral data.

Secondary, or targeted, intervention strategies are provided for students who need more behavioral support than universal or primary prevention. These interventions usually increase (1) adult supervision and assessments; (2) adult–student interactions, especially positive reinforcement; (3) administration of a common and more intensive strategy to a relatively small group of students; (4) emphasis on the function or purpose of a student's problem behavior; and (5) daily data collection, analysis, and feedback (Crone, Horner, & Hawken, 2004).

Similarly, tertiary, or intensive, intervention strategies are provided for students who do not respond to targeted or secondary interventions. These strategies are highly individualized, function-based (consider the purpose or consequences of behavior), linked to targeted social skills training, and closely adult supervised (Crone & Horner, 2003). The effects of secondary- or tertiary-level interventions on student behavior can be assessed in several ways and are discussed in depth within other chapters of this book (e.g., systematic direct observation, direct behavior ratings, behavior rating scales). The key is in determining which behavioral monitoring tool is most appropriate for a given situation in order to provide the best information for decision making.

Using Data to Guide Decision Making and Action Planning

Schools that effectively implement SWPBS processes emphasize the use of data-based decision making to guide their action planning processes. As discussed in Chapter 1, data that are collected continuously (progress monitoring purposes) allow decision making to be current and action planning to be efficient and relevant. The remaining sections of this chapter provide guidance on the effective, efficient, and relevant use of whole school data such as office discipline referrals.

WHAT ARE THE GUIDELINES FOR WHOLE-SCHOOL ASSESSMENT AND MONITORING?

In the whole-school context, behavioral assessment and monitoring are important to enhance the accuracy, efficiency, and relevance of the implementation of the above SWPBS characteristics. Because the array of information that is potentially available for collection at the whole-school level is variable in complexity, availability, and usefulness, we suggest that school teams apply the following guiding principles to enhance the efficiency and relevance of the assessment process.

Start by Developing the Questions That Need to Be Answered to Improve Important Academic and Behavioral Outcomes

To promote regular data collection and use, data must be associated with relevant school questions that are (1) linked to short- and long-term outcome priorities of the school and (2) improve and inform practice and teaching. Assessment questions should guide and shape the data collection and monitoring procedures. At the universal or primary prevention tier, when interventions are broadly targeted at *all* students, SWPBS schools routinely consider the first five questions in Table 2.1. However, individual schools might be interested in other questions based on the characteristics and needs of their school, such as those listed in items 6–12.

Start with Existing Data Sources

Before investing in new data collection procedures or methods, schools should look at what data are routinely collected at the classroom and schoolwide levels. Most schools monitor and collect information, for example, on absences and tardies, minor and major rule violations, awards earned, discipline referrals, days in attendance, credits earned, suspensions and expulsions, and referrals for special supports. Although each of these data sources could be used as an example of schoolwide data collection, we focus on office discipline referrals (ODRs) because of their availability in schools and the increased amount of attention they are receiving in the research literature. Specifically, a number of researchers have demonstrated that ODRs can be useful for decision making if definitions are clear, referring processes are standardized, staff are supported in the accurate use of these processes, and procedures for imputing and summarizing these data are efficient (Horner & Sugai, 2001; Irvin et al., 2004, 2006; Sprague, Sugai, Horner, &

TABLE 2.1. Examples of Typical Whole-School Behavioral Questions

	Schedule
Standard whole-school questions	
1. What is the average number of discipline referrals (major, minor, both) logged per day in a given month?	Monthly
2. How many instances of each type of rule-violating behavior (e.g., fighting, noncompliance, late to class) have been processed per month and year?	Monthly
3. Where have most discipline referrals occurred (e.g., hallway, bus, classroom)?	Monthly
4. When during the day have most discipline referrals occurred (e.g., 10:30, 12:00, 3:15)?	Monthly
5. How many discipline referrals have been earned by individual students (e.g., 12 students with 6 or more, 30 students with 2–5, 121 students with 1, and 333 students with 0)?	Monthly, quarterly, annually
Examples of other whole-school questions	
6. How many discipline referrals were given by individual staff members?	Quarterly
7. What proportion of students by ethnicity received a discipline referral in comparison to proportion of students by ethnicity enrolled in the school?	End of year
8. What proportion of students received zero or one major discipline referral?	End of year
9. How many students have three or more unexcused absences?	Any time
10. How many incidents of harassment were reported by grade level?	Quarterly, annually
11. How many suspension incidents, days of suspension, students who earned at least one suspension consequence, etc?	Quarterly, annually
12. What function or motivation seemed to be associated with the five times that "Elizabeth" has received a behavior incident report for using profanity in the hallway?	Any time

Walker, 1999; Sugai, Sprague, Horner, & Walker, 2000; Tobin, Sugai, & Colvin, 1996; Wright & Dusek, 1998). Although in most public schools teachers are expected to manage minor disciplinary incidents in the classroom (e.g., being out of seat, talking out of turn), they are encouraged to complete ODRs when they believe that a student's behavior should be addressed by someone outside of the classroom, as in the case of high-intensity behavior (e.g., violent physical behavior) or recurring behaviors (e.g., repeated noncompliance during class period). In most cases, ODRs are processed by a building administrator (e.g., principal, assistant principal), who then decides how to respond to the incident (e.g., parent conference, suspension) (Wright & Dusek, 1998).

HOW DO YOU USE WHOLE-SCHOOL DATA COLLECTED FROM ODRs?

Use a Consistent Form

To facilitate the collection of discipline referral data, schools commonly use a "discipline referral" slip or form to record information about the rule violation. The contents and data requested on this form should be consistent with behavioral definitions, discipline referral procedures, and so forth. A generic example of a behavior discipline reporting form is displayed in Figure 2.2. An important aspect of this form is the section in which the referring staff person provides a general hypothesis for the purpose or function of the observed problem behavior. This hypothesis is used to inform the type of consequence that is assigned to the rule-violating problem behavior. If a problem behavior is maintained by escape from adult attention, keeping a student at school may be more effective than assigning an out-of-school suspension. When a student receives discipline referrals, information such as function, behavior, location, and time of day can reveal patterns that serve as a preliminary functional assessment for behavior intervention planning (tertiary level). In Case Example 2.1, we illustrate the use of such data in individual assessment.

Collect, Input, Summarize, and Evaluate Data as Events Occur and When Questions Need to Be Answered

If data are going to be used for decision making at the whole-school level, procedures for collecting and summarizing information must be simple, logical, and time efficient. In the next chapter, we provide further discussion and examples of ways to use existing data, particularly at the secondary and tertiary levels. Data are not likely to be used for formative or ongoing decision making if, for example, information is entered into a database at the end of each month, construction of graphs requires expertise in the use of spreadsheets or databases, schools must depend upon district-level summarization and display of data, large amounts of irrelevant data or many displays must be reviewed and sifted, or data are not displayed in visually simple and informative graphic formats.

When school teams develop or invest in systems for tracking discipline data, they should assess whether (1) information can be entered quickly and as part of the process of reviewing the event with the student (e.g., 30 seconds per event), (2) data summaries can be obtained immediately after information has been entered (e.g., in less than 1 minute), (3) visual displays to answer standard evaluation questions can be obtained through simple "clicks" instead of entering data formulas to create tables and graphs, and (4) at least two staff members are fluent in data entry and management procedures. An example of such a system can be seen under "demo" at *www.swis.org/*.

Graphic displays and visual analysis of information allow for more immediate recognition of relative changes and patterns. In Figure 2.3, the same sample of discipline data is displayed in two different formats: tabular and graphic. The data being represented are the same; however, data patterns are more salient in the graphic than the tabular form. In Chapter 8, we review several available options for visually analyzing data that are presented in graphic form.

Although the graph in Figure 2.3 is helpful in displaying the data, trends over time are not visually obvious because each school month has a different number of school days. For example, for the above school, December and March have school breaks of 2 weeks, meaning that some months have fewer (or more) opportunities for students to engage in rule-violation behavior. Thus, in Figure 2.4, the number of school days in each month has been divided into the number of discipline referrals, producing a rate: number of discipline referrals per day per month. This display of the same data indicates that rates of discipline referrals in August, December, and March are relatively high.

Behavior Incident Report	
Student _____ Grade _____ Date _____ Time _____ Homeroom Teacher _____ Referring Staff _____	**Location** ☐ Classroom ☐ Hallway ☐ Classroom ☐ Cafeteria ☐ Library ☐ Bathroom ☐ Bus ☐ Assembly ☐ _____

Problem Behavior	**Possible Motivation** **(Check one)**	**Administrative Decision**
Minor (Give to Homeroom Teacher) ☐ Inappropriate Language ☐ Defiance ☐ Classroom Disruption ☐ Misuse of Property ☐ Teasing ☐ Tardy ☐ Out of Assigned Area ☐ Other _____	☐ Obtain Peer Attention ☐ Obtain Adult Attention ☐ Obtain Items/Activities ☐ Avoid Peer(s) ☐ Avoid Adult ☐ Avoid Task/Activity ☐ Unclear ☐ Other _____	☐ Loss of Privilege ☐ Time in Office ☐ Conference with Student ☐ Parent Contact ☐ Individualized Instruction ☐ In-School Suspension (____ hours/days) ☐ Out-of-School Suspension (____ days) ☐ Other _____
Major (Give to Office Staff) ☐ Repeated Noncompliance ☐ Physical Aggression ☐ Harassment ☐ Stealing ☐ Tobacco or Banned Substance ☐ Off Campus w/o Permission/Truant ☐ Dress Code ☐ Other _____	**Others Involved (Check one)** ☐ None ☐ Peers ☐ Staff ☐ Teacher ☐ Substitute ☐ Supervisor ☐ Bus Driver ☐ Other _____	**Comments Descriptions**

Signatures		
_____	Referring Staff Person	Date _____
_____	Administrator	Date _____
_____	Student	Date _____
_____	Parent/Guardian	Date _____

FIGURE 2.2. Generic example of complete discipline referral form.

CASE EXAMPLE 2.1

Claudette is a third-grade student who has received seven office discipline referrals over the past 3 months. An examination of three of Claudette's last seven discipline referrals (one of which is shown below) suggests that she is most likely to display disruptive behavior during classroom activities that involve difficult work (function = escape from difficult work). Her other four discipline referrals involve noncompliance with adults in the hallways and cafeteria (function = get adult attention). The student assistance team uses this information to develop an individualized behavior support plan consisting of two main behavior teaching objectives: (1) teach behaviors that allow her to escape difficult work when in class (e.g., "I have done as much as I can for now") and (2) teach behaviors that give her access to adult attention that is contextually appropriate (e.g., "Can I tell you something that happened?").

Behavior Incident Report	
Student Claudette Grade 3 Date October 12 Time 9:00 Homeroom Teacher Ms. Wilbur Referring Staff Ms. Wilbur	**Location** ☑ Classroom ☐ Hallway ☐ Classroom ☐ Cafeteria ☐ Library ☐ Bathroom ☐ Bus ☐ Assembly ☐ _____

Problem Behavior	Possible Motivation	Administrative Decision
Minor (Give to Homeroom Teacher) ☐ Inappropriate Language ☐ Defiance ☐ Classroom Disruption ☐ Misuse of Property ☐ Teasing ☐ Tardy ☐ Out of Assigned Area ☐ Other _____	**(Check one)** ☐ Obtain Peer Attention ☐ Obtain Adult Attention ☐ Obtain Items/Activities ☐ Avoid Peer(s) ☐ Avoid Adult ☑ Avoid Task/Activity ☐ Unclear ☐ Other _____	☐ Loss of Privilege ☐ Time in Office ☐ Conference with Student ☑ Parent Contact ☐ Individualized Instruction ☐ In-School Suspension (___ hours/days) ☐ Out-of-School Suspension (___ days) ☐ Other _____

Major (Give to Office Staff)	Others Involved (Check one)	Comments/Descriptions
☑ Repeated Noncompliance ☐ Physical Aggression ☐ Harassment ☐ Stealing ☐ Tobacco or Banned Substance ☐ Off Campus w/o Permission/Truant ☐ Dress Code ☐ Other _____	☑ None ☐ Peers ☐ Staff ☐ Teacher ☐ Substitute ☐ Supervisor ☐ Bus Driver ☐ Other _____	This is the third time this month that Claudette has yelled and torn up her assignment in front of the class.

Signatures

_____	Referring Staff Person	Date	_____
_____	Administrator	Date	_____
_____	Student	Date	_____
_____	Parent/Guardian	Date	_____

Tabular Display   Graphic Display

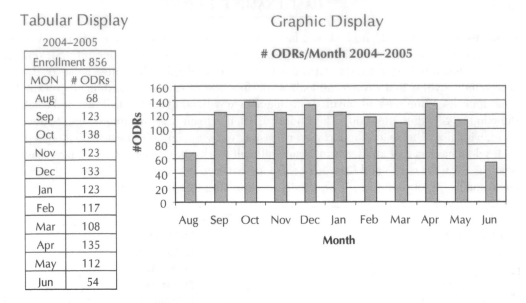

2004–2005

Enrollment 856	
MON	# ODRs
Aug	68
Sep	123
Oct	138
Nov	123
Dec	133
Jan	123
Feb	117
Mar	108
Apr	135
May	112
Jun	54

FIGURE 2.3. Tabular versus graphic displays of data.

After controlling for the effects of different number of school days across school months, review of discipline referral patterns across months becomes more accurate and informative. Most school leadership teams then begin to ask additional questions about their data:

- What rule-violating behaviors did students display (Figure 2.5)?
- Where did students display these behaviors (Figure 2.6)?
- When were students most likely to receive a discipline referral during the school day (Figure 2.7)?
- Which students received more than three discipline referrals (Figure 2.8)?

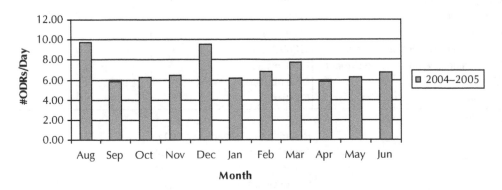

FIGURE 2.4. Number of discipline referrals per day per month.

When reviewing data to answer these questions, school leadership teams must remember that each office discipline referral is affected by whether the student engages in the behavior (or gets caught), whether the staff person correctly processes the event (or processes it at all), and whether the administrator processes and inputs the event into the database. Thus, any interpretation of responsibility and/or recommendation for change must consider the combined effect of the student, the staff person, and the administrator who were involved in the discipline referral event.

Individual schools may see differences in the kinds of behaviors that result in discipline referrals; however, this specificity of information gives leadership teams the opportunity to be strategic when identifying and adopting interventions. For example, an assessment of the data in Figure 2.5 indicates that the most common discipline referral was for inappropriate use of language, followed by disruptions, tardies, noncompliance, and dress code. The data summary in Figure 2.6 clearly indicates that most discipline referrals are originating from the classroom, with a number of referrals distributed relatively equally but at lower rates across a number of nonclassroom settings (e.g., hallways, cafeterias, gym, common areas, and bus loading).

The graph in Figure 2.7 provides a display of the discipline referral distribution across 15-minute intervals of the school day. Data patterns indicate "spikes" or noticeable increases in the number of referrals in and around morning and afternoon recess/break and during transitions associated with the three overlapping grade-level lunch periods. Viewing the data collected as a whole, a leadership team can focus the development of their SWPBS action plan on disruptions and inappropriate use of language that are occurring in the classroom and nonclassroom settings, especially around morning, lunch, and afternoon transitions. This plan might focus on teaching what appropriate and respectful language sounds like in these settings, increasing the amount and quality of adult supervision, and increasing levels of positive reinforcement for responsible language and behavior in these settings.

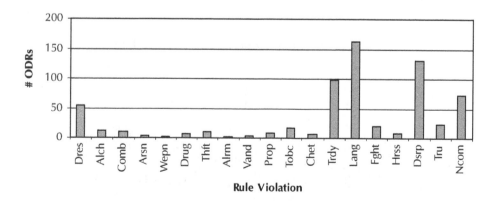

Major Discipline Referrals by Behavior to Date

FIGURE 2.5. Number of major discipline referrals by behavior. Dres, dress code violation; Alch, alcohol use/possession; Comb, possession of combustible item; Arsn, arson; Wepn, possession of a weapon; Drug, drug use/possession; Theft, theft; Alrm, Bomb threat and false alarm; Vand, vandalism; Prop, property damage; Tobc, tobacco use/possession; Chet, cheating; Trdy, tardy; Lang, inappropriate language; Fght, fighting; Hrss, harassment; Dsrp, disrespect; Tru, truancy; Ncom, noncompliance.

Major Discipline Referrals by Location to Date

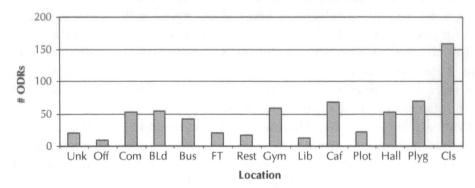

FIGURE 2.6. Number of major discipline referrals by location. Unk, unknown; Off, office; Com, common area; Bld, bus loading; Bus, bus; FT, field trip; Rest, restroom; Lib, library; Caf, cafeteria; Plot, parking lot; Hall, hallway; Plyg, playground; Cls, classroom.

Looking at the general patterns of discipline referrals at the whole-school level provides school leadership teams with the opportunity to narrow and refine how they develop action plans for supporting all students and staff across the whole school. Because many times some students require more behavior support than available in schoolwide universal or primary systems, school leadership teams must organize their screening and intervention resources to address the more individualized behavioral needs of these students. In addition, early discipline-related problem behavior can predict later negative school outcomes (Tobin & Sugai, 1999a, 1999b; Tobin et al., 1996; Tobin, Sugai, & Colvin, 2000). Data at the whole-school level can serve as a starting point for identifying which students might need more intensive behavior supports. For example, in Figure 2.8, the students who have received 3 or more major discipline referrals are sorted, representing 40 students (or roughly 5%) of the 856 in the school. Three students have 20 or more discipline referrals, 7 have between 10 and 20, 15 students have between 5 and 10, and 15 have between 3 and 4. In general, two

Major Discipline Referrals by Time to Date

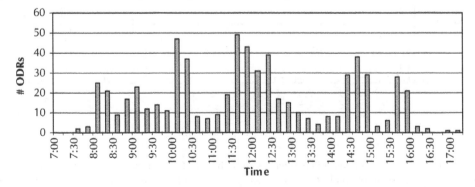

FIGURE 2.7. Number of major discipline referrals by time.

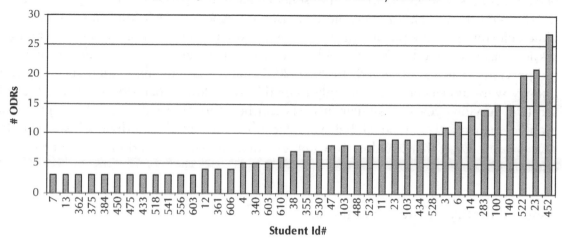

FIGURE 2.8. Students with three or more major behavior incidents.

main questions are considered: (1) What can we do to enhance and intensify behavior supports for the group of 40 students who have 3 or more discipline referrals (secondary-tier interventions)? and (2) what can we do now for those students who are unresponsive to secondary-tier interventions and/or have 6 or more discipline referrals (tertiary-tier interventions)?

To improve how schools self-assess the status of their SWPBS implementation, school leadership teams should look at their whole-school data within and across school years. The sample graph in Figure 2.9 presents data for three years: 2004–2005 (before a change in the schoolwide discipline system), 2005–2006 (after initial adoption and implementation of SWPBS), and 2006–2007 (second-year implementation of SWPBS). In this case, a school leadership team can see that their first-year implementation (2005–2006) seemed to have an initial impact on number of discipline referrals

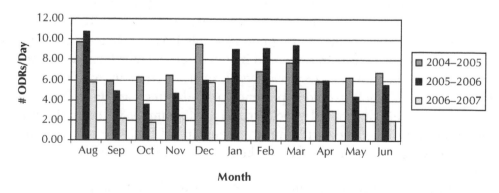

FIGURE 2.9. Number of discipline referrals per day per month across 3 years.

between August and December of the school year in comparison to preimplementation (2004–2005). However, a noticeable increase was experienced in the number of discipline referrals per day per month in January, February, and March. A booster training session was conducted in March, and a concurrent decrease to rates similar to those of the previous year was observed. In 2006–2007, improved implementation accuracy and fluency were associated with monthly rates that were lower than observed in either of the two previous years. A similar analysis can be conducted with any of the previous graphic displays (i.e., type of behavior, location, time of day, individual student) to reveal information that could narrow implementation decisions and enhance behavioral outcomes.

Assess Fidelity of Implementation

The accuracy, timeliness, and usefulness of all data-based decisions are linked to the extent to which data assessment and monitoring procedures are implemented efficiently, accurately, and consistently. The old adage of "garbage-in, garbage-out" is applicable to whole-school data information systems. To assess the accuracy of their implementation, effective SWPBS teams regularly review behavior definitions, procedural fidelity, and decision-making processes and outcomes. The questions in the self-assessment in Appendix 2.1 focus on elements that affect the accuracy of implementation of behavioral assessment and monitoring at the whole-school level. In Case Example 2.2, we provide one example of how the self-assessment might be utilized.

Evaluate from a Systems Perspective

The above guidelines enable school teams to collect and use behavioral data at the whole-school level effectively, efficiently, and relevantly. To evaluate from a systems perspective means to consider the whole school, that is, all students and all staff across all school settings. First order change indicators (e.g., rates of problem behavior, use of suspensions) have been the focus of this chapter. However, second-order change indicators (i.e., social and educational validity; Schwartz & Baer, 1991; Wolf, 1978) also are important to measuring the impact of whole-school efforts. Recently, SWPBS implementation efforts have taken into account the potential impact of these programs in terms of gains in administrative and instructional minutes (Scott, 2001; Scott & Barrett, 2004). For example, if a school reduced its major discipline referrals from 1,234 to 613 (–50%) in one school year, the school administrator would recoup over 15 eight-hour days, using a conservative estimate of 15 minutes to process each referral. From an instructional perspective, the school as a whole would experience a 58-day increase in instructional time, assuming that the student is out of the classroom for 45 minutes for each discipline referral. Due to the gains associated with improvements in SWPBS, the school administrator has more time to be an instructional and school leader, and students have access to more instructional time.

The self-assessment in Appendix 2.2 might be used by school teams to guide their whole-school evaluation process. In Case Example 2.3, we illustrate how the self-assessment might be utilized to assess the process of intervention implementation.

CASE EXAMPLE 2.2

New City Middle School began implementing a schoolwide positive behavior support (SWPBS) program at the beginning of the school year. As the final days of school approach, the school's PBS team is interested in assessing how far the school has come over the past 8 months as well as what issues they still need to work on. The team meets after school to review and discuss the self-assessment questions found in Appendix 2.1.

After discussing each of the 16 questions, the team determines that the school has two main issues to focus on in preparation for the coming school year, related to the following three self-assessment questions:

1. Have clear distinctions been established between administrator- versus staff-managed rule violations?
9. Has a schedule been established for regular collection and summarization of data?
10. Has a schedule been set for regular team meetings to review data and answer a small set of whole-school evaluation questions?

Through their discussion, the first issue that the team recognized was that they had not done a good job of establishing a schedule. The assistant principal had been designated the sole person in charge of managing and summarizing data, and he had waited until a day or two before each team meeting to attend to the data. One problem was that the team meetings had been scheduled somewhat haphazardly (e.g., four times in the month of September, but no meetings in November). As a result, there were some months in which the schoolwide data went unexamined. The second concern that arose was the fact that several classroom teachers were continuing to refer students to the principal's office for what the team considered to be minor, classroom-managed offenses (e.g., tardiness, out of seat). Although the team had outlined the differences between minor and major rule violations during an inservice day at the beginning of the school year, it became clear that it was necessary to further review this information with the teachers who were still unclear about it (thus providing some secondary-level support).

CASE EXAMPLE 2.3

After the students returned from vacation in January, there was a rise in the number of discipline referrals for disruptive/inappropriate behavior on the playground at Pine Tree Elementary School. The school's leadership team decided to implement an intervention on the playground that consisted of (1) training playground supervisors in active supervision (e.g., moving, scanning, and interacting with students) and (2) providing behavior-specific praise when students were doing what was expected of them on the playground. Prior to beginning the intervention, the team completed a self-assessment to better guide their implementation (see Appendix 2.2). In order to ensure that the intervention was being implemented with accuracy by all playground supervisors, the team decided to conduct random observations on the playground twice a week (implementing an intervention item #1) and record the resulting data (implementing an intervention item #2). If they found that playground supervisors were being more passive than active in their supervision, supervisors would participate in a more intensive training session (implementing an intervention item #3). Lastly, the principal committed to reviewing the discipline referral data weekly to assess whether the intervention was having an effect on disruptive/inappropriate playground behavior (implementing an intervention item #4). The team agreed that if the intervention did not produce a noticeable decrease in discipline referrals at the end of a 3-week period, they would reconvene to modify the intervention plan.

WHAT ARE THE STRENGTHS OF USING ODR DATA?

Easily Accessible/Already Available

Most schools already collect data on disciplinary infractions because the information is needed at the district and state levels to track disciplinary activity and disposition decisions. Given that it is already collected, these data are highly feasible and minimally intrusive for use in assessment. However, as previously noted, the procedures for summarizing information must be simple, logical, and time efficient.

Useful in Describing and Assessing School Climate

Assuming that schoolwide disciplinary practices and procedures have been standardized and are consistently applied to all students, enforced by all staff, and considered for all school settings, these data provide a descriptive measure of whole-school safety and social climate. For example, if a few students have high rates of rule-violating behavior, individual behavior intervention plans are indicated. In contrast, if a large number of students are involved in the schoolwide discipline system, schoolwide practices and procedures (i.e., systems) need to be examined. If context information (e.g., location, time of day, type of problem behavior, possible function) is collected, relevant and specific interventions can be put in place.

Easy for Stakeholders (e.g., Teachers) to Use

Schoolwide discipline data give each faculty member a means of participating in whole-school improvement efforts. Schools that use data to guide their leadership team planning can develop interventions that are relevant to the unique features of their school, and can convince school staff to participate in activities that build organizational consistency and effective communications at the whole-school level.

WHAT ARE THE WEAKNESSES OF USING ODR DATA?

Potential Time Consumption

Although more information is sometimes perceived as better, in the case of whole-school data assessment and monitoring, more is not always better. Sustained implementation will be difficult to achieve if the data assessment and management process is cumbersome and unwieldy. As described previously, school teams should focus on (1) a small number of specific questions that are aligned with clear and measurable outcomes; (2) processes for input, manipulation, and summarization of information that are built into the operation of the discipline process and consume no more than 1% of staff time; (3) adopting software technologies that minimize the manipulation of information and the establishment of advanced technology skill sets; and (4) decisions that are linked to specific and context-relevant questions. A general guiding principle is to produce a small number of relevant and efficient data displays that enable immediate interpretation and response.

Focus on Rule Violations and Problem Behaviors

Clearly, schools pay attention to problem behavior because it intrudes on the functioning of instructional and nonclassroom activities and because districts and states typically require reporting of discipline incidents and dispositions. However, this emphasis can lead to excessive consideration and use of relatively aversive consequences and distract attention from teaching and encouraging prosocial student behaviors. Change in discipline referral rates can tell what students are not doing wrong as often, but not what they are doing well. Thus, our goal should be to shift attention from discipline data as a negative characteristic of a school and toward using this information to improve behavior support from the whole school and to the individual student.

Difficulty in Establishing and Maintaining Consistent and Accurate Use by Individual Teachers and Administrators

Challenges in implementation might be linked to poor definitions, lack of skill fluency, absence of agreement about what constitutes a referral, or lack of effective classroom and behavior management techniques. And, it should be noted that even when these challenges have been addressed, the psychometric properties of the measures have generally been unstudied and thus are unknown (Wright & Dusek, 1998). The greater the extent to which a school leadership team can establish agreements about common definitions, policies, and procedures, the more useful the data can be in facilitating whole-school decisions. Finally, attention to potential observer drift may need to be addressed through periodic retraining.

Misinterpretation

Inappropriately high rates of discipline referrals are often associated with negative evaluations of teacher competence and effectiveness. On the surface, low rates can be interpreted as good (i.e., teachers are good behavior managers), whereas high rates are seen as bad (i.e., teachers lack good classroom management skills). In the latter situation, administrative assistance and even sanctions can result. However, it is important to remember that each behavior incident involves more than student behavior (good or bad). Local norms for judging acceptability (context related), teacher response (appropriate or inappropriate), and administrator involvement and processing (appropriate or inappropriate) also define the interaction and determination of who is "at fault."

CONCLUDING COMMENTS

The purpose of this chapter was to review behavioral assessment and monitoring strategies and procedures that could be applied to efficient and effective data-based decision making at the whole-school level. Although our examples focused on social behavior assessment using ODRs, a similar approach can be applied to school content areas such as literacy, sciences, art, and music. In general, the process begins with specification of contextually relevant questions as a way to determine what data are needed. If these questions are clearly stated, identifying what data need to be collected to answer the question should be relatively straightforward. Whole-school data, such as ODRs, may be used across all purposes of assessment (screening, diagnostic, progress monitoring, and evaluation), especially at the primary intervention level. Although supplemental data may be needed, whole-school data can provide important contextually relevant information when engaging in assessment at the secondary or tertiary levels.

The bigger challenge for schools is the establishment of data collection, storage, and summarization procedures that are effective, efficient, and contextually relevant. Data systems that involve cumbersome data input, long waits for data outputs, and difficult-to-interpret data displays are not feasible, and thus are unlikely to be used and maintained. If behavioral assessment and monitoring procedures work well, whole-school evaluation is more likely to be regular, frequent, relevant, and continuous.

ENHANCING ACCURACY OF WHOLE-SCHOOL BEHAVIORAL SELF-ASSESSMENT AND MONITORING

For each item, circle either "Yes" or "No."

1	Have clear distinctions been established between administrator- versus staff-managed rule violations?	Yes	No
2	Is a proactive comprehensive schoolwide discipline system being implemented?	Yes	No
3	Are rule violations clearly defined?	Yes	No
4	Has a complete behavioral incident recording form been developed (e.g., discipline referral, behavioral incident) for documenting rule violations?	Yes	No
5	Are positively stated and behaviorally defined student expectations in place?	Yes	No
6	Has a written schoolwide discipline policy been written?	Yes	No
7	Are procedures and systems in place for storing and maintaining data?	Yes	No
8	Is a school leadership team in place to coordinate behavioral assessment and monitoring and to lead problem solving and needs assessments?	Yes	No
9	Has a schedule been established for regular collection and summarization of data?	Yes	No
10	Has a schedule been set for regular team meetings to review data and answer a small set of whole-school evaluation questions?	Yes	No
11	Has a person been designated to manage, maintain, summarize, and graph data on a monthly basis?	Yes	No
12	Are data decision rules in place for evaluating data and making intervention decisions?	Yes	No
13	Does the leadership use the data to develop data-based recommendations for their action plan?	Yes	No
14	Does the team have opportunities to present, discuss, modify, and establish an action plan with staff?	Yes	No
15	Are procedures in place for monitoring the accuracy and consistency of implementation of action plan activities?	Yes	No
16	Are procedures in place for modifying features of the action plan based on the data?	Yes	No

WHOLE-SCHOOL BEHAVIORAL SELF-ASSESSMENT

For each item, circle either "Yes" or "No."

	CONSIDERING AN INTERVENTION		
1	Are data that we used to identify a need reliable/accurate?	Yes	No
2	Do we have agreement about the importance and priority of the need?	Yes	No
3	Does an intervention exist that purports to address the need?	Yes	No
4	Does evidence exist to support the claims of the intervention?	Yes	No
5	Do we know of other schools that have been successful in their use of this intervention?	Yes	No
6	Does evidence exist to suggest that this intervention is contextually and socially relevant to our situation?	Yes	No
7	Is this intervention logistically doable in our situation?	Yes	No
8	Can the intervention or practice be modified/adapted for the unique features of our situation?	Yes	No
9	Can staff be trained and prepared effectively and efficiently to use the intervention in our situation?	Yes	No
	IMPLEMENTING AN INTERVENTION		
1	Are data being collected on a regular schedule on the accuracy of implementation of the intervention?	Yes	No
2	Is the intervention or practice being implemented with accuracy in all required settings and situations?	Yes	No
3	Are supports available to ensure durable and accurate implementation of the intervention over time?	Yes	No
4	Are procedures and structures in place to frequently and regularly assess the effectiveness and efficacy of the intervention implementation?	Yes	No
	EVALUATING IMPACT OF THE INTERVENTION		
1	Are criteria available for judging the adequacy of the behavioral impact and social validity of the intervention?	Yes	No
2	Is adequate progress being made toward addressing the stated need?	Yes	No
3	Do students, staff members, parents, and/or community members judge the intervention and its outcomes as being adequate?	Yes	No
4	Can modifications be made to the intervention to improve outcomes?	Yes	No
5	Can modifications be made to improve the efficiency of the intervention implementation?	Yes	No
6	Can elements of the intervention be eliminated while still maintaining desired outcomes?	Yes	No
7	Do students, staff members, parents, and/or community members support continued use of the intervention?	Yes	No
8	Are minimum procedures and structures in place to maintain achieved effects and outcomes?	Yes	No

3

Using Extant Data
in Behavioral Assessment

WHAT ARE EXTANT DATA AND WHY USE THEM?

In Chapter 2, we discussed types of information that are often collected at the schoolwide level. For example, ODRs are routinely collected within schools and can provide useful information at all levels of behavioral assessment. In this chapter, we extend this discussion to other sources of extant data that might also be already available, yet whose use in assessment may not be readily apparent—for example, permanent products. These extant data are often readily available and informative about previous patterns of behavior but may be overlooked as a valuable data source.

These types of data are important for a variety of reasons. First, this information can complement more formal assessment tools in providing a comprehensive picture of a student. That is, these data can serve an informative role in multimethod, multisource, multisetting assessment practices by offering a contextual source of information that might be missed in the use of standardized, norm-referenced measures. Second, these data often are collected in a formative fashion, that is, ongoing or collected repeatedly over time, so they serve as an excellent tool in progress monitoring. For example, a teacher who records student performance on weekly spelling quizzes can review those data to reveal error patterns (e.g., "*i* before *e* except after *c*" rule not mastered). This source of outcome data could then be used to document the effectiveness of an intervention with the goal of mastering this rule. Third, and perhaps most importantly, extant data serve as a readily available source of data. As noted in Chapter 1, a challenge of conducting behavioral assessment and monitoring in applied settings is achieving a balance between precision and feasibility. As reported by Alberto and Troutman (2006), another advantage of using extant data is that the products are permanent—that is, we can review the data either on an ongoing basis or at a later time.

Although these characteristics may be appealing, a disadvantage of ex post facto analysis of data is insufficient information to appropriately analyze a problem. For example, simply examining the grade recorded (percent correct) on weekly math quizzes over the past month does not provide information on how students attempted to solve problems, or if interfering problem behaviors were present (e.g., peer distractions, difficult tasks). These additional types of information often are not collected and reported while the student is actually engaged in the task.

WHAT TYPES OF EXTANT DATA MIGHT BE AVAILABLE FOR ACADEMIC BEHAVIORS?

A variety of permanent products are available for academic behaviors, for example, videotapes, audiotapes, computer logs, or, most commonly, paper-and-pencil formats. Richards, Taylor, Ramasamy, and Richards (1999) noted that various paper-and-pencil type products are readily available in schools. For example, teacher grade books, homework, and student report cards represent forms of academic data that are routinely recorded by teachers. Academic permanent products may be grouped into two categories: (1) performance summaries, such as scores recorded in a teacher grade book and results of district or state norm-referenced testing, and (2) work samples, such as worksheets, writing assignments, or art projects. See Table 3.1 for additional examples.

Performance Summaries

Performance summaries are available sources of academic data that are typically already aggregated and presented in a "formal" format, for example, grades on quizzes and tests recorded in a teacher's grade book, quarterly progress reports, and results of district/ state-level assessments. However, to be useful for making instructional decisions, these data must be organized in meaningful ways. In one situation, for example, this may mean graphing weekly or monthly grades on math homework assignments to understand the frequency with which a student has attained a goal of 85% correct or better. In another situation, it may mean organizing yearly state-mandated testing scores or end-of-year grades in specified subjects over the past 3 years into a single table to provide a global, long-term picture of academic performance.

TABLE 3.1. Examples of Possible Extant Data for Academic Behaviors

Academic permanent products	Examples
Work samples	• Worksheets • Homework • Daily journals • Writing assignments • Art projects • Portfolios
Performance summaries	• Grades on quizzes and tests • Other information recorded in teacher grade books (e.g., number of homework assignments completed) • Progress reports • Results of district/state-level assessments • Results of curriculum-based measurement

Enhancing the meaning of these types of data begins with an overall record review. See Appendices 3.1–3.3 for examples of forms that may be useful in organizing extant data. Completed examples of these forms are provided in Figures 3.1, 3.2 (in Case Example 3.1), and 3.3 (in Case Example 3.1).

Although permanent products may provide an excellent source of everyday data for academic behaviors, the challenge is identifying what data to use and how often. Nearly all teachers use grade books to input and organize student data; yet, little is done with this information after it is recorded. Many teachers only look at the recorded grades when computing averages at the end of a grading period. However, a grade book can be an extensive database for ongoing monitoring of performance at the individual student or whole-class level. For example, graphing grades on a simple chart can provide a useful picture of how individual students, or the class as a whole, are doing academically. In addition, teachers can chart student progress before and after the introduction of a new instructional technique to visually determine its effectiveness. In Case Example 3.1, we further illustrate this point.

RECORD REVIEW

Date: 1/20/2006

Student's Name: Ellie Martin

Grade: 5

Student's overall level of performance/progress (circle one):   Typical
(Below progress/performance expected)   Above progress/performance expected

> **Background/Health Information:** Ellie's family recently moved, causing her to change schools midyear (from South to North Elementary School). Ellie's file shows that she received a referral to the Planning and Placement Team at her former school due to problems with attention. Although the team tried to implement a prereferral intervention, Ellie's family moved before the team was able to see any results.

> **Academic Information:**
>
> **Reading:** For the past 2 years, Ellie has received C's on progress reports.
>
> **Writing:** Ellie generally receives grades in the B–C range.
>
> **Math:** Ellie's progress reports reveal a mixture of A's and B's.
>
> **Results of Standardized Testing (fill in name of measure used and relevant scores):**
>
> _X_ **District/State-Level Assessment:** CTBS (Comprehensive Test of Basic Skills): Reading (45th percentile), Writing (55th percentile), Mathematics (80th percentile), Science (72nd percentile), Social Studies (65th percentile)
>
> **Aptitude Testing:** _____
> _____
>
> **Achievement Testing:** _____
> _____

FIGURE 3.1. Example of a completed record review form.

CASE EXAMPLE 3.1

Mr. Jones is a third-grade teacher at Sunnydale Elementary School. Over the past two weeks, the focus of his math lessons has been on multiplication. Every other day, Mr. Jones gives his students a 2-minute timed quiz involving single-digit multiplication problems. Although there has been a range of student performance on these quizzes, Mary has had particular trouble, often scoring at or below 40% correct. Mary's mother, Mrs. White, meets with Mr. Jones to discuss what she can do to help her daughter learn the multiplication tables. After much discussion, Mrs. White agrees that she will spend 15 minutes each night reviewing multiplication flash cards with Mary. They plan to meet in 2 weeks to determine whether Mary has made any progress.

As Mr. Jones gives math quizzes and tests to his class, he records each of Mary's scores on a permanent product recording sheet (Figure 3.2). In preparation for meeting with Mrs. White, Mr. Jones plots each of Mary's quiz scores on a simple chart presented in Figure 3.3.

In reviewing the data together, it was clear that the supplemental time spent reviewing the flash cards at home had been worthwhile. Although Mary started off answering fewer than half of the problems correctly, by the end of the second week she had scored an 83% on her test. Very pleased with the results, Mrs. White decided to continue reviewing the flash cards with Mary every night after dinner but also asked Mr. Jones if there was anything else she could do to help Mary. Simply by looking at the test scores, however, Mr. Jones was unable to recall what specific types of errors Mary had made. In order to find this out, it was necessary for Mr. Jones to turn to the actual work samples.

PERMANENT PRODUCT RECORDING SHEET

Date(s): September 7

Student's Name: Mary

Subject: Math

Behavior: Math problems solved correctly

Permanent Product: Weekly math quizzes & tests

Date	Type of Permanent Product	How Many Times Behavior Occurred	Total Opportunities for Behavior to Occur	Percentage of Observed Behavior (Observed/Total × 100)
10/1	Math test #1	8	20	40%
10/7	Math test #2	10	20	50%
10/10	Math quiz	5	10	50%
10/14	Math test #3	15	20	75%
10/21	Math test #4	15	18	83%
10/25	Math quiz	8	10	80%

FIGURE 3.2. Example of a completed Permanent Product Recording Sheet.

(continued)

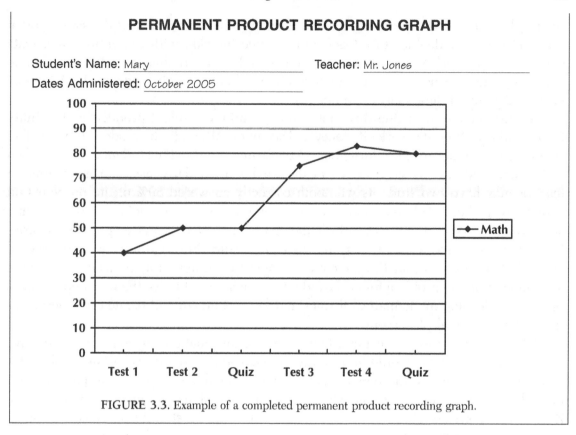

PERMANENT PRODUCT RECORDING GRAPH

Student's Name: Mary   Teacher: Mr. Jones

Dates Administered: October 2005

FIGURE 3.3. Example of a completed permanent product recording graph.

Although grade books are most often used to record academic performance information, they can also be used to track information about a student's social behavior. Participation rating (e.g., high, medium, low engagement) or measures of appropriate or inappropriate behavior (e.g., number of conflicts avoided, time out of seat) can enhance the usefulness and meaningfulness of extant information (see additional discussion later in this chapter).

Work Samples

Another source of academic data comes from work samples, such as daily homework, worksheets completed during independent work time, writing assignments such as a daily journal, and creative arts projects such as drawing or building with blocks. Howell and Nolet (2000) described work samples as a way to keep a student's actual behavior in a portfolio. These sources of data are often used by teachers to determine the overall scores or grades discussed in the previous section on performance summaries; however, they also can and should be used to provide specific information about the reason for a particular problem or success—such as the information needed when engaging in diagnostic assessment. For example, review of the types of errors made on previous math quizzes reveals that Susie has not mastered basic facts for multiplication by four. A review of quizzes for the entire class even suggests that more than half the class had the same type of error. The teacher decides to reteach and practice the skill with the entire class. Data obtained from work samples can be summarized in a graphic format to determine whether progress is adequate or if an instructional change is indicated (see the Appendix for a discussion of data analysis strategies).

Another benefit of taking this approach to examining student products is the ability to determine a student's work efficiency and accuracy. Although the grade at the top of an assignment provides useful information, determining the way the student approached an assignment and the types of errors made can be particularly useful. For example, a teacher may have two students who both correctly answered 50% of the problems on a math worksheet. Whereas one student worked slowly and deliberately and only answered the first half of the questions, the other student quickly attempted every problem but made consistent errors in decimal placement. Both earned the same overall grade, but certainly not for the same reason—and thus different approaches are needed for remediating the problem for each student. A teacher might give the first student more practice to develop mathematical fluency and the second student explicit instruction on the rule for decimal placement.

Work samples can be an important source of information for conducting an error analysis, which, in turn, would inform reteaching. The type of error analysis employed is generally dependent on the type of skill being examined, and a variety of questions can be addressed (see Table 3.2). The Multilevel Academic Skills Inventory (MASI; Howell, Zucker, & Moorhead, 2000) exemplifies one tool that can assist in the analysis of errors in the subject areas of mathematics, reading comprehension, decoding, language, written expression, social skills, and task-related skills. For example, in the area of mathematics, the MASI can be used to identify several possible errors, including sign errors (i.e., student uses the sign incorrectly), missing steps (i.e., student fails to borrow or regroup correctly), and incorrect algorithms (i.e., added both the numerator and denominator). Although error patterns in work samples can be examined without use of a reference tool such as the MASI, the use of such a tool can simplify the process and make apparent previously unconsidered types of errors. An example of an error analysis for mathematics is provided in Case Example 3.2.

TABLE 3.2. Questions to Consider When Conducting an Error Analysis

- Have I chosen a measure that provides sufficient opportunities for errors to occur?
- Have I encouraged the student to try all problems and to show his or her work?
- Have I tried to get as many examples of meaningful errors as possible (by reviewing products on which the student was only partially correct or those that illustrate her best efforts)?
- Have I tried to better understand the student's processes by noting patterns in his or her errors?
- Have I tried to categorize errors or corrects by content, behavior, condition, or thought process (fact, concept, rule, strategy)?
- Have I noted and categorized skills that the student did not demonstrate?
- Have I asked the student "How did you arrive at this answer?"
- If and when I thought that I found an error pattern, did I see if I could confirm it by predicting the sort of error a student would make and then giving a specific assessment to see if the pattern occurs?

Note. Based in part on Howell and Nolet (2000).

CASE EXAMPLE 3.2

Let's return to the case of Mary and her multiplication tables. After his parent–teacher conference with Mary's mother, Mr. Jones returned to his desk to more closely examine Mary's last multiplication test in order to identify additional areas upon which interventions might be focused. Although Mary was performing at a significantly higher level since she began reviewing the multiplication facts at home, her rate of improvement had slowed over the past couple of quizzes. Mr. Jones wondered whether there was a specific skill (or skills) that Mary still lacked. In order to answer this question, he chose to conduct an error analysis. Results of Mary's last test are presented below:

MATH TEST #4

Student's Name: Mary   **Date:** October 21

3	2	6	9	4	6
$\times 4$	$\times 5$	$\times 7$	$\times 8$	$\times 4$	$\times 1$
12	10	42	72	16	6

3	7	8	5	9	3
$\times 9$	$\times 2$	$\times 1$	$\times 6$	$\times 2$	$\times 3$
72	14	8	30	18	9

8	3	1	6	2	7
$\times 5$	$\times 2$	$\times 4$	$\times 3$	$\times 6$	$\times 9$
40	6	4	18	3	36

When Mr. Jones reviewed the test, his first inclination was to examine whether all of Mary's mistakes involved the same number (which would indicate that Mary and her mother should devote extra time to reviewing those particular facts). However, he found that the three problems that she answered incorrectly (3×9, 2×6, and 7×9) all involved different digits, so he examined the problems more closely. On the first and last problems, it appeared that Mary multiplied correctly, but simply reversed the digits in her answer (i.e., $3 \times 9 = 27$ written as 72). The other error Mary made was in multiplying correctly but then adding the digits together in her answer (i.e., $2 \times 6 = 12$, $1 + 2 = 3$). When Mr. Jones then looked back at Mary's previous quizzes, he found several of the same errors. Although she did not make these errors consistently, Mr. Jones decided that it would be worthwhile to devote extra instructional time to reviewing digit placement in multiplication.

Curriculum-Based Assessment

Given its planned and purposeful use in academic assessment and monitoring, *curriculum-based assessment* (CBA) is not typically used as a permanent product source of information. However, CBA information can serve a useful purpose in performance summaries and as work samples. For example, CBA data can be summarized and aggregated to provide evaluative and normative information about overall performance within or across individuals, classes, or entire schools. Although norm-referenced standardized tests may be useful for measuring long-term progress, these measures are generally not designed

for use in frequent repeated assessment. In contrast, CBA data can provide a specific picture of (1) what kind of performance should be expected from students in a particular
environment, (2) what types of error patterns exist, and (3) whether students need specialized or remedial instructional supports (i.e., at-risk screening purposes). Most CBA
approaches involve measures that can be quickly and repeatedly administered to a select
individual or group for progress monitoring, selecting appropriate intervention, and
using a response-to-intervention model.

Hintze, Christ, and Methe (2006) indicate that CBA actually represents a number of
diverse assessment practices but is commonly defined to include measurement activities
that incorporate direct recording of performance in the local curriculum for informing instructional decisions. The manner in which the curriculum is sampled to create the
assessment items differentiates one CBA approach from another. For example, in the general outcome measurement approach, items from across the entire year might be sampled
in one model. In contrast, specific subskill mastery measurement approaches involve
sampling items from a particular aspect of the curriculum. See Hintze and colleagues
(2006) and references in Table 3.3 for further information about the characteristics, simi-
larities, and differences of various CBA methods.

Curriculum-based measurement (CBM) is an example of a general outcome measurement approach to CBA that fits into a three-tier model of assessment. For example, when an
entire school adopts CBM, the performance of all students might be assessed three times
per year to obtain normative information for the entire school (i.e., primary prevention
level). The performance of those students who are found to be at risk for academic difficulty
(i.e., secondary prevention level) is assessed monthly to ensure that effective instruction is
being provided. Students whose performance does not improve sufficiently would receive
specialized and individualized instruction and be assessed on a weekly basis (i.e., tertiary
prevention level). In general, the more intensive the instructional need, the more frequently data are collected to inform student progress and instructional decision making.

The following example illustrates this CBA approach to response to intervention: Mr.
Green has recently begun implementation of an academic intervention intended to
increase the speed (fluency) with which a group of students can recite multiplication
tables. Mr. Green wants to know if the intervention is effective and worth the extra implementation effort. Using percent correct (accuracy) would not provide information about
student fluency (number correct per minute). In addition, weekly quiz administration is
insufficient to inform day to day intervention decisions. Mr. Green changed to 2-minute
CBM probes involving multiplication facts, which were administered twice a week over a
3-week period. This more timely and specific information improved his assessment of
student learning and teaching effectiveness.

WHAT TYPES OF EXTANT DATA MIGHT BE AVAILABLE FOR SOCIAL BEHAVIORS?

A multitude of permanent product and extant data sources are available for assessing and
intervening with social behaviors at the schoolwide, classwide, and individual student
levels. First, as discussed at length in Chapter 2, data obtained from ODRs provide a use-

TABLE 3.3. Useful Resources for Additional Information on Curriculum-Based Assessment/Curriculum-Based Measurement

Resource	Descriptor
AIMSweb: *www.aimsweb.com*	AIMSweb allows users to access CBM probes for use in reading, mathematics, spelling, and writing. After scores are electronically entered into the AIMSweb web-based database, it is easy to summarize and graph results to be reviewed online or printed out. The cost to use the AIMSweb database is about $1 per student per year.
Dynamic Indicators of Basic Early Literacy Skills (DIBELS): *dibels.uoregon.edu*	This website by the University of Oregon allows users to download DIBELS assessment materials addressing fluency in seven domains of reading (initial sounds, letter naming, phoneme segmentation, nonsense word, oral reading, retell, and word use). In addition, DIBELS data can be electronically entered into the web-based database in order to produce both graphs and automated reports. The cost to use the DIBELS database is about $1 per student per year.
Intervention Central's Curriculum-Based Measurement Warehouse: *www.interventioncentral.org*	The curriculum-based measurement warehouse provides a wide assortment of materials for learning about and conducting CBM. CBM assessment materials and administration manuals are available for reading, math, spelling, and writing. Users can also create probes for each of these four content areas. The website's ChartDog tool converts electronically entered CBM data into progress monitoring graphs. In addition, materials are available to help train large groups of teachers and other educators in CBM. All materials on the Intervention Central website are currently free.
Academic Skills Problems Workbook (Shapiro, 2004)	The final three chapters in this workbook are dedicated to progress monitoring, particularly CBM. In the first chapter, the authors provide guidance and practice in creating and visually analyzing graphs. The second chapter is dedicated to describing how educators can develop local norms (i.e., individual classroom, school) for measures such as CBM. Finally, the development and use of goal charts is discussed.
Curriculum-Based Measurement (Shinn, 1989) *Advanced Applications of Curriculum-Based Measurement* (Shinn, 1998)	These books contain chapters by several authors focusing exclusively on CBM. In addition to providing background information about what CBM is and when it should be used, subsequent chapters discuss several uses of CBM and research regarding CBM. Administration and scoring procedures are also addressed.
The ABCs of CBM: A Practical Guide to Curriculum-Based Measurement (Hosp, Hosp, & Howell, 2007)	This book is part of the *Practical Interventions in Schools* series by The Guilford Press. As such, it presents accessible information and hands-on instruction for conducting curriculum-based measurement (CBM) in grades K–8 and then using the information to make sound decisions regarding instruction and intervention. In addition, the role of CBM within a response-to-intervention model is explained.

ful source of information for social behavior. For example, the principal of East Middle School is concerned about the number of fights occurring among seventh-grade students, especially in nonclassroom settings. To determine specifically where to increase levels of active supervision, the principal reviews ODRs for the last 2 months and learns that most fighting incidents are occurring outside the cafeteria and in the bus loading area. With this information, the principal organizes school resources to increase adult proximity and active supervision in those nonclassroom locations.

Although it may not be sufficient for assessment at the individual student level, ODR data can be used to screen for students in need of further assessment and provide a context for a student's level of behavior within the school. For example, ODR information may describe generally what school rules a student's behaviors have violated and where these problems behaviors occurred, but more is needed to develop individualized behavior intervention plans (e.g., antecedent and consequence events, possible function, setting of events, time of day, routines, etc.). Additional examples of social behavior measures are illustrated in Table 3.3.

Other sources of schoolwide social behavior information include attendance and tardy records and academic progress indicators, such as quarterly grades. Attendance and tardy information can reveal students who have a variety of social behavior challenges, for example, poor health, lack of transportation, avoidance of academic failure, competing social distractors (e.g., friends), and work outside of school. The resulting information can assist teachers, parents, counselors, and school psychologists to develop more effective and relevant behavior support plans.

A growing body of research evidence supporting this link between academic difficulties and problem social behavior (see Lane, O'Shaughnessy, Lambros, Gresham, & Beebe-Frankenberger, 2002; Torgesen et al., 1999; Trzesniewski, Moffitt, Caspi, Taylor, & Maughan, 2006) confirms that academic sources of information can be important in informing the development of behavior support plans. A quarterly review for students who have a dramatic decline in their academic grades can reveal, for example, that they have experienced a significant change in their school, family, or community situation or are not benefiting from the instruction that is being provided. Through early intervention with instructional accommodations and/or behavioral supports, the occurrence of problem behaviors and future risk status might be reduced.

Existing behavior management plans implemented at the individual, classwide, and/or schoolwide levels represent another important source of information for decision making. For example, most effective educational environments include a clearly articulated plan for promoting positive behavior, commonly in the form of a token economy. In turn, the distribution and trade-in of tokens (e.g., points, certificates, tickets) for displays of appropriate social behaviors (e.g., sharing, taking turns, problem solving, being on time) represent excellent sources of information for evaluating the effectiveness of schoolwide or classroomwide behavior management systems. This information can be used to approximate rates at which (1) school staff are acknowledging appropriate student behavior at appropriate rates and (2) students are displaying appropriate school and classroom appropriate behaviors.

Similar assessments and evaluations can occur at the classroom and individual student levels. Teachers commonly establish classroom management systems that involve teaching typical classroom routines, strengthening cooperative group behaviors, and managing classroom rule violations. When systems are established to collect information on number of teacher acknowledgments and reprimands, teachers can evaluate the effectiveness of their overall instructional and behavior management practices and the general status of student behavior in their classrooms

When students require individualized behavior interventions (e.g., targeted social skills instruction, behavioral contracts, function-based behavior support plan), data are usually collected on the students' behavior in relation to the effectiveness of those interventions. ODRs, attendance patterns, tokens earned, and other information can be used at the individual student level. In addition, assessment decisions can be facilitated by examining information available in current and/or previous intervention plans. For example, Mr. Lane refers one of his eighth-grade students, Joe, to the student support team for "inattention." When the team asks Mr. Lane if he has tried any interventions with Joe, he describes a self-monitoring program using a direct behavior rating (DBR) in which Joe is asked to evaluate how well he had been paying attention. The team immediately identifies DBR information as potentially useful in assessing Joe's behavior. When the school psychologist reviews these data, she can determine what behaviors might be important to observe during a classroom visit to evaluate whether changes are needed in the current behavior intervention plan.

Data collected outside of the school setting may also be helpful. For example, Ms. Klein has worked with John's father to establish a consistent homework routine to increase John's homework completion rates and academic achievement. Since beginning this intervention, John's father has kept a log each night of the time John spends on his homework. Together, Ms. Klein, John, and John's father can use this information to evaluate whether instruction needs to be modified and/or his homework routine is effective. Examples of other types of data for informing decisions related to social behavior can be found in Table 3.4.

Whether at the schoolwide, classroom, or individual student levels, the data need to be collected, summarized, and analyzed on a regular schedule. For example, if a token economy is established and the number of tokens are not counted and reviewed on a weekly basis, determining intervention effectiveness and making timely adjustments will not be possible.

TABLE 3.4. Examples of Possible Extant Data
for Social Behaviors

- Data from current and/or previous attempted intervention plans
- Office discipline referrals
- Reward slips/prize tickets
- Suspension/expulsion records
- Request for assistance forms
- Health records
- Records of meetings held about the student
- Class absences
- Direct behavior ratings

HOW DO YOU DECIDE WHICH INFORMATION MIGHT BE USEFUL?

Given the variety of existing data types, the next question is to determine which information might be most useful in decision making. The general answer will depend on why the data are needed, or what available data would best match the existing problem. To facilitate answering this question, a number of guidelines should be considered.

First, extant data must be easily accessible in a timely manner to those individuals who use the information to make decisions. From an efficiency perspective, extant data have the advantage of already existing; however, it is important to determine if the data are readily accessible. For example, information might not be helpful if grade scores are archived in a password-protected file, or confidentially policies restrict access to individual student data.

Second, extant data should be clearly organized and easily summarized. Even if data are accessible, how much the data have to be manipulated and reduced will affect their usefulness. For example, information that must be collected from each student's personal file, compiled and sorted from a box in which behavior slips have been accumulating for the year, or submitted by individual teachers and then summarized are examples of systems that are costly with respect to time, effort, and personnel.

Third, the existing data must be trustworthy and accurate to be useful in decision making. If teachers and office staff do not agree on what should be referred to the office, tokens are not disseminated in the same way by all staff, or information fields on behavior incident reports are left blank, then these information sources lose their value and usefulness in decision making.

Finally, at least one person, but preferably a team, must have the time, expertise, and capacity to use summarized data to guide decision making. The most accurate, accessible, and summarizable data are useless if they cannot be used to guide instructional and behavioral decisions that improve outcomes for students and quality of interventions.

HOW DO YOU SUMMARIZE DATA COLLECTED?

As discussed in Chapter 2, a prerequisite to being able to summarize extant data is to determine what is considered a correct versus an incorrect response. For example, if Mrs. Smith considers not raising a hand before responding worthy of an ODR but Mr. Jones completes discipline referrals only for physical altercations, counting the number of referrals in one week will not provide an accurate picture of behavior in the school. The need to develop specific, operationalized definitions of correct and incorrect behavior becomes particularly important when more than one individual works with a student. However, even if a student spends most of the day with a single individual, time spent clearly identifying what constitutes the problem behavior is necessary to make certain everyone agrees when discussing student behavior. Different perceptions and levels of tolerance about problem behavior exist and affect how we interpret or rate student behavior. However, to the greatest extent possible, school staff should strive for consensus on what constitutes prosocial (correct) versus problematic (incorrect) behavior.

Once agreement has been established, a number of possibilities for summarizing data are available. In fact, Richards and colleagues (1999) provide a nice review of available options for summarizing data collected via what they refer to as permanent products. In Case Example 3.3, an illustration is provided of how one might utilize methods of summarization with regard to extant data, including:

- *Frequency count.* One of the easiest ways to summarize data is to keep a running tally of how many times the behavior occurs. For example, a principal may be interested in how many times a particular student has been late to school over the past month. Two conditions must be met when using a frequency count. First, a similar number of opportunities must be possible for the behavior to occur across time (e.g., spelling problems, opportunities to be called upon). Second, the length of each observation session must be equal, for example, five tardies in five days would be interpreted differently from five tardies in five months). If these conditions are not met, rate or percentage (correct/incorrect) is calculated.

- *Rate.* Rate is calculated as a way to standardize a frequency count by dividing the number of observed responses by the length of the observation. In the academic realm, we are used to seeing rates (e.g., number of words read correctly per minute, number of assignments completed in a week). An example of a rate calculated for a social behavior would be the number of tokens a student has earned for positive behavior per week. Rates, however, can be artificially inflated or deflated if the number of opportunities to

---

CASE EXAMPLE 3.3

It is only October and Dr. Clark, the school psychologist, has already received multiple referrals regarding a 10th-grade student, Luke, because of struggles across academic areas. On the last progress report, Luke received D's in all of his core content classes (e.g., English, history, science, math, foreign language), which was not consistent with his academic performance in previous years. Although Luke had not been an A student in the past, he had consistently received a mixture of B's and C's.

Dr. Clark approaches each of Luke's teachers and asks them to compile some information for him. First, he asks for a frequency count of the number of times that Luke has been absent from their classes each week since the beginning of the school year. Second, he asks each teacher to calculate a percentage (rate) of the number of homework assignments that Luke has completed thus far (Dr. Clark asks for a rate in case teachers did not assign homework every night). Third, he asks for the results (in percentages) of any quizzes or tests that Luke has taken in each class. Last, he asks each teacher to share a copy of his or her syllabus, including information regarding how grades are calculated.

Once Dr. Clark receives the requested information, he sits down to summarize and evaluate it. He is surprised to find that Luke has earned satisfactory grades on his quizzes and tests (typically B's and C's). What then catches his eye, however, is the fact that Luke has been absent an average of two days a week in each of his classes. In addition, he has only completed approximately 33% of the total number of homework assignments. When Dr. Clark looks at Luke's course syllabi, he discovers an important piece of the puzzle: Across subjects, both homework and class participation (e.g., discussion, presentations, science labs) contribute significantly to the overall course grade. Dr. Clark quickly realizes that efforts must focus on identifying factors that are affecting Luke's attendance and how those problems can be overcome.

respond are exaggerated or restricted, respectively. Richards and colleagues (1999) indicate that fewer than 10 response opportunities can affect rate accuracies. Although a shorter time period can be selected to provide an estimate of behavior (e.g., 5 minutes), teachers must ensure that the period will accurately represent the overall rate of behavior. See Case Example 3.1 for an example of summarizing and graphing data using rate (blank forms can be found in Appendices 3.2 and 3.3).

• *Cumulative responses.* Recording the cumulative number of responses is similar to conducting a frequency count. However, rather than recording number or rate of behavior for individual observation sessions, a running total or cumulative record of the number of behaviors is maintained. For instance, a high school principal might reward students who receive an accumulated total of 10 positive referrals with a special parking spot in the campus lot.

• *Trials to criterion.* Recording the number of trials to criterion is particularly relevant when assessing skills that are still being learned (i.e., acquisition phase). The number of responses that an individual makes before reaching a performance criterion on the target behavior is emphasized. For example, a student learning to throw a basketball into a hoop will probably make several attempts before succeeding. In determining the number of trials to criterion, we are interested in how many shots it takes before the basket is made. Or a student learning to independently follow a recipe may successfully complete only half of the recipe instructions independently. In such a case, trials to criterion would be expressed as a percentage (50%) of the steps completed.

WHAT ARE THE STRENGTHS ASSOCIATED WITH USING EXTANT DATA?

Easily Accessible/Already Available

Perhaps the greatest strength of extant data relates to their ready availability. As noted by Noell, Duhon, Gatti, and Connell (2002), information gleaned from permanent products can be collected throughout the day without placing any additional burden on the classroom teacher, such as remembering to conduct ratings at specific intervals or to collect assessment information while engaged in other classroom responsibilities. Additionally, time pressure is relieved, in that it is possible to review the products at a later time.

Reduced Risk of Reactivity

As noted by Noell and colleagues (2002), collection of permanent product data can reduce the risk of reactivity, which is the likelihood for an individual to display atypical behavior in the presence of an outside observer. A basic example of reactivity occurs when an external observer enters the classroom to observe a student with disruptive behavior, and the student does not act out because she knows that she is being watched. With permanent products, typically the classroom teacher is simply utilizing already existing data and is not altering the classroom environment in a way that students would notice. Therefore, reactivity would be diminished.

Contextually Relevant

Another strength of extant data is insight into the everyday functioning of student behaviors that are most relevant to the classroom teacher. Because the data often are taken from existing sources, they provide a picture of student behavior that is relevant to the particular classroom or school. In addition, since these outcome measures are typically selected by the classroom teacher, they should be more socially valid. Data from sources like standardized tests or systematic direct observation are often not relevant to the immediate classroom or instructional context.

WHAT ARE THE WEAKNESSES ASSOCIATED WITH USING EXTANT DATA?

Could Easily Become Time Consuming

Although the time required for data collection can be dramatically reduced when using extant data, the process of summarizing the data has the potential to become time consuming. In addition, if an error analysis is conducted, the process could be significantly lengthened. One important step toward ensuring efficiency is to determine which data are necessary to answer the questions posed. As noted in Chapter 2, when summarizing data, efficient systems for data display must be used. For example, if data are graphed, an easy graphing tool such as ChartDog should be utilized (see *interventioncentral.org*). Guidelines regarding graphing are addressed in more depth in the Appendix at the end of this book.

May Paint a Limited Picture

As is the case with any assessment tool, extant data may not be useful in all situations. Because preexisting sources of data are being used, an accurate representation of what the student knows or can do may not be possible. In these types of situation, an assessment would not reveal an entire picture of a student's skills, and this type of data should not be used in isolation, particularly when making high-stakes decisions such as those related to placement or diagnosis. Extant data should be one part of a multimethod assessment practice.

Difficulty in Establishing and Maintaining Consistent and Accurate Use

For extant data to be useful, consistent and accurate use must be established. For example, if a school contains four classrooms in the same grade, it is highly unlikely that those four teachers will utilize identical grading systems. Teacher A might base 50% of a student's grade on homework, whereas Teacher B might base 25% of a grade on homework. A similar problem exists for social behaviors, such as when two teachers possess different tolerance levels for misbehavior. Although this weakness is not of as much concern when assessing student performance within the classroom, it is an important consideration when making interclassroom comparisons or assessing at the whole-school level.

Unknown Psychometric Adequacy

Wright and Dusek (1998) highlight the point that when ODRs are constructed, focus is rarely placed on issues of psychometric adequacy (e.g., reliability, validity). Likewise, with most forms of extant school data (the exception most often being norm-referenced standardized tests), psychometric properties have not been investigated. For example, few teachers probably put their math tests through statistical analyses to ensure that they are reliable and valid.

CONCLUDING COMMENTS

In this chapter, several options are presented for using assessment data that already exist in schools but may be overlooked. Potential sources of extant data for academic and social behavior were reviewed, along with how those data might be used across various assessment purposes. The use of extant data is appropriate for a particular situation if the need for using this information is clear and the particular type of needed data is clear. The primary advantage of using extant data is its feasibility, that is, it already has being collected. In other words, the use of existing data can reduce the burden on data collection resources and enhance the goodness of fit within the natural environment. Riley-Tillman and Chafouleas (2003) indicate that using existing systems is more likely to be implemented and sustained with integrity and acceptability. However, caution must be exercised when using extant data, particularly regarding the need for an efficient method of summarizing the data and the potential limitations for use in high-stakes decisions.

RECORD REVIEW

Date: _____

Student's Name: _____

Grade: _____

Student's overall level of performance/progress (circle one):   Typical

Below progress/performance expected   Above progress/performance expected

Background/Health Information:

Academic Information:
Reading:
Writing:
Math:

Results of Standardized Testing (fill in name of measure used and relevant scores):
___ District/State-Level Assessment:

Aptitude Testing: _____
_____
_____

Achievement Testing: _____
_____
_____

PERMANENT PRODUCT RECORDING SHEET

Date(s): _____

Student's Name: _____

Subject: _____

Behavior: _____

Permanent Product: _____

Date	Type of Permanent Product	How Many Times Behavior Occurred	Total Opportunities for Behavior to Occur	Percentage of Observed Behavior (Observed/Total × 100)

PERMANENT PRODUCT RECORDING GRAPH

Student's Name: _____   Teacher: _____

Dates Administered: _____

Comments: _____

_____

_____

_____

_____

_____

_____

_____

_____

_____

_____

_____

_____

_____

_____

4

Systematic Direct Observation

SDO (circled, handwritten annotation)

purpose (handwritten annotation in left margin with bracket)

In previous chapters, we focused on methods of collecting data from highly feasible sources. Although such assessment sources are important to comprehensive behavioral assessment, in some cases we need to know exactly what is happening in a classroom at a particular time. In these situations, it is appropriate to turn to the form of behavioral assessment that can provide a "snapshot" of an environment at a specific time. In this chapter, various techniques for conducting systematic direct observation (SDO) are reviewed, along with procedural guidelines and examples supporting each technique. Next, guidance is provided in selecting behaviors and techniques, and then summarizing data. Finally, general strengths and weaknesses of using SDO are discussed.

WHAT IS SDO AND WHY USE IT?

At its most basic level, direct observation refers to having some observer watching an environment for some period of time. The data from this observation typically include some verbal or written record of what was observed. When conducting direct observations of student behavior, it is important to specify the type of observation technique utilized. One group of procedures involves naturalistic observation, which is characterized by entering a setting and observing behavior without prior selection of behaviors to observe (Hintze, Volpe, & Shapiro, 2002). The observer could enter a classroom during morning math instruction and record behaviors as they occur, later summarizing them to provide a complete description of behaviors and context. The detail with which behavior is recorded may vary from a global description of an event (e.g., "Sally pushed Mike") to a narrow, more specific descriptive recording involving context as well as antecedents and consequences (e.g., "During recess today, Sally pushed Mike to the ground after he told her that she was not good at playing hopscotch").

Although naturalistic observation techniques have the potential to provide important information depending on the reason for conducting the observation, these techniques also have drawbacks that can limit their application in behavior assessment and monitoring. The lack of a predetermined, specified behavior and associated standardized definition does not permit the combining of data across observations to produce a reliable and valid record of specific behavior over time. In addition, narrative observation techniques are highly vulnerable to inferential judgments and to greater variance from observer to observer (Sattler, 2002). Given the difficulty inherent in quantifying the data, information gathered from naturalistic observation might be helpful in initial identification and analysis stages of problem solving but may not be useful in monitoring behavior over time or across settings.

As noted above, SDO is a method that allows an observer to take a snapshot of a student's behavior as well as of the whole environment over some defined time period. This is done by selecting detailed methods of coding what an observer sees during an observation period. In contrast to naturalistic observation, SDO refers to observation of explicit behavior that is predefined and collected in prespecified settings. Salvia and Ysseldyke (2004) indicated five characteristics that distinguish SDO from naturalistic approaches.

1. The reason for observation is to measure specific behaviors.
2. These behaviors have been defined in operational terms.
3. The data are collected under standardized procedures that allow for a high level of objectivity.
4. The time and place for observations are specified and selected.
5. Data are scored and summarized in a standardized fashion and thus do not vary from observer to observer.

These five characteristics increase our confidence in the resulting data. Being specific regarding what is being observed and standardizing the procedures and presentation of the data enhance confidence that the data are representative of the student's behavior. For example, Sammy may have been referred by his teacher for not paying attention in class. After further discussion, the teacher and school psychologist decide that the behavior is most likely to occur during independent seatwork. Thus, observation sessions are scheduled to collect baseline information during those times, with the behavior to be observed defined as academic engagement. Further specification of academic engagement is needed (Shapiro, 1996), so the teacher decides to mark the target behavior as present if Sammy is either passively (e.g., listening to a lecture, reading silently) or actively (e.g., writing, raising hand) engaged. A standardized system for collecting data about Sammy's academic engagement is specified, and the school psychologist agrees to summarize the information prior to their next meeting.

As discussed by Hintze et al. (2002), the rationale for use of SDO over other procedures lies in the need to gather relevant information about students using reliable and valid assessment practices. Given our emphasis on assessment practices that can serve multiple purposes, including capacity for progress monitoring, support for the use of SDO procedures is emphasized in this chapter.

WHAT ARE SPECIFIC TECHNIQUES FOR SDO?

There are different versions of SDO, with each presenting unique strengths and weaknesses. Selection of a particular technique begins by operationally defining the behavior or group of behaviors of interest and specifying the question(s) that need to be answered about the behavior. In general, the first step is to define the beginning (onset) and end (offset) of a behavior or group of behaviors. This information is essential in order to know when to count or measure the length of an event. Three ways to think about grouping behaviors might be selected for SDO. First, behaviors can be discrete—that is, behaviors that are similar in appearance (topography) across events (e.g., hits, profanity, touches, words read correctly). Second, behaviors can be behavioral chains, which are sequences of related individual behaviors that represent a larger unit of behavior (e.g., problem solving, adding multiple three-digit numbers). Third, behaviors can be grouped by behavior or response classes, which refer to groups of topographically different behaviors that are similar in their function (i.e., purpose or maintaining consequence). For example, teasing to access peer attention could be verbal, physical, and/or gestural, and accessing teacher attention could be hand raising, calling out, or going to the teacher.

You can determine which SDO observation method to use based on (1) how often and how fast behaviors are occurring, (2) the extent to which the observer can record the occurrences, and (3) what questions need to be answered. In general, SDO techniques fall under one of two categories: event based or time based (Wolery, Bailey, & Sugai, 1988). Event-based techniques involve directly recording each behavior occurrence to determine

- *Frequency*—number of events in a period of time (e.g., four hits in a 6-hour day).
- *Rate*—number of events per unit of time (e.g., 24 words read correctly per minute).
- *Duration*—total time (e.g., actively engaged in reading for 12 minutes), percent of time (e.g., out of seat for 35% of the reading period), average time per event (e.g., each temper tantrum lasted an average of 7.5 minutes).
- *Latency*—time for behavior to begin after prompt or antecedent cue provided (e.g., on average 2 minutes to begin task after teacher direction given).
- *Permanent product*—counting the outcomes or products of behavior (e.g., number of math problems completed on a worksheet during a 45-minute math session). (See Chapter 3 for more detail.)

In contrast, time-based techniques are selected when event based systems are difficult to conduct, such as when (1) behaviors are occurring at rates that are too fast to count accurately (e.g., profanity during a temper tantrum), (2) individual behaviors vary in duration (e.g., 20 seconds out of seat vs. 15 minutes out of seat), or (3) observers are unable to continuously observe multiple behaviors or students or behaviors of a group of students (e.g., teaching while observing, keeping track of multiple behaviors). In time-based techniques, data are recorded during prespecified intervals of time within a specified observation session and then are summarized into percentage of intervals of behavioral occurrences and nonoccurrences. Unlike event-based systems, in which each behavioral event is observed, time-based methods result in approximations because behavioral occurrences are assessed at specific intervals of time. Behavioral events are sampled in one of three basic ways:

- *Momentary time sampling*—behavioral occurrence is indicated if behavior occurs at and only at the end of an observation interval.
- *Whole-interval recording*—behavioral occurrence is indicated if behavior occurs during and only during the whole duration of an observation interval.
- *Partial-interval recording*—behavioral occurrence is indicated if behavior occurs at least once at any time within an observation interval.

In the next section, a review of each method is provided, and a summary of each technique is presented in Table 4.1.

Event-Based Recording

Use of an event-based technique is a good choice when the target behavior is relatively discrete, that is, relatively short in duration, each behavioral event is equal in duration,

TABLE 4.1. Summary of Strengths and Weaknesses of Direct Observational Recording Procedures

Method	Question addressed	Example	When to use/not to use
Event-based recording			
Frequency	How many times did the behavior occur?	Johnny talked out of turn 10 times during a 20-minute interval.	DO use if behavior has clear beginning and end. DON'T use for continuous or infrequent behaviors, or if you need to know about duration or intensity.
Duration	How long did the behavior occur?	Johnny was out of his seat for 5 minutes.	DO use to measure elapsed time. DON'T use if behaviors do not have clear beginning and end.
Latency	How much time elapsed between a signal and the response to the signal?	30 seconds elapsed between the point at which Mrs. Smith asked Johnny to stop talking and when he stopped talking.	DO use to measure elapsed time. DON'T use if behaviors do not have clear beginning and end.
Time-based recording			
Whole interval	Does the behavior occur during the entire interval?	Johnny fidgeted in his seat during the entire 15-second interval.	DO use for continuous behaviors. DO NOT use for infrequent behaviors. CAUTION: may underestimate true occurrence of behaviors.
Partial interval	Does the behavior occur at any time during the interval?	Johnny fidgeted in his seat for some duration of time during the 15-second interval.	DO use for low-frequency but lengthy behavior (provides time to record). CAUTION: may overestimate true occurrence of behavior.
Momentary time sampling	Does the behavior occur at a specified time?	Johnny fidgeted in his seat during the first second of the 15-second interval.	DO use to observe several behaviors simultaneously and to conduct peer comparisons (provides time to record). CAUTION: may miss infrequently occurring behavior.

and logistics permit continuous observations. In general, this category of techniques is focused on counting behavioral occurrence or nonoccurrence within a specified observation session. As mentioned above, event-based systems also involve answering questions about the duration and/or latency of a behavior.

Frequency and Rate

This event-based technique requires a simple tallying or counting of each behavior occurrence during the specified observation period and place. For example, you might count the number of times Sam raises his hand during whole-class math instruction. This recording can simply be done using a pencil and paper. Other event recording methods include moving a rubber band from one wrist to the other, using a frequency counter "clicker," and making a small rip on the edge of a card or piece of paper. Frequency count data are summarized by totaling the number of times the behavior occurred. If the observation period is always the same length (e.g., 48-minute science period), the direct counts can be presented (e.g., 4 hand raises on Monday, 3 on Tuesday, 9 on Wednesday, 0 on Thursday). If the observation period varies in length, however, rate is calculated by dividing the number of observed events by the length of the associated observation period (e.g., 2 talk-outs per minute on Wednesday, 0.5 talk-outs per minute on Thursday, 3 talk-outs per minute on Friday). To facilitate interpretation, event-based data can be graphed in bar or line graphs (see Figure 4.1). In Chapter 3, an example of converting frequency to rate for academic data can be found in Case Example 3.1.

A frequency count summary can be made across the entire observation period or broken into smaller intervals that represent the observation period, such as every 15 minutes during morning instructional activities. One advantage to breaking the period into intervals is that patterns of behavior across time can be examined. To enhance the contextual meaning of event data, additional information could be collected, for example, (1) information about the setting (e.g., curriculum, number and kinds of peers, physical arrangements), (2) antecedent stimulus events that precede behavioral events (e.g., teacher directives/instruction, peer behaviors), (3) consequence stimulus events that follow behavioral events (e.g., teacher or peer attention, removal of instructional materials, being removed from the room), and (4) nonroutine stimulus events or conditions (called "setting events") that affect the value or influence of typical antecedent and consequence events (e.g., illness, social conflict, missed medications).

In addition, information about the distribution of behavioral events can be obtained by further dividing an observation session into smaller observation intervals. For example, a 40-minute observation session could be subdivided into eight 5-minute intervals, and as events occur, they are tallied within the appropriate 5-minute interval. The result is a general pattern of the distribution of behavioral events across the observation setting. Yet another tactic is to subdivide the school day into meaningful intervals. That is, if tantrums are the target behavior, a tally mark could be made within the daily planner for each occurrence. This procedure may pinpoint times the behavior is most likely to occur, such as just before lunch or immediately following gym class. Another way to break an observation period into intervals is through use of a scatterplot (a blank scatterplot can be

In the past 2 weeks, Sammy, a third-grade student, has been throwing tantrums during the day. Sammy's teacher, Mrs. McIntyre, is concerned by this behavior and seeks the guidance of the school psychologist. Although she promises that she will be in to observe Sammy as soon as possible, the school psychologist asks Mrs. McIntyre to keep a *frequency count* of how many times Sammy tantrums over the next few days. Mrs. McIntyre agrees to keep a tally throughout the entire school day (8:00–2:30), and then the school psychologist will graph the data using a bar chart. Mrs. McIntyre's data are provided below:

Day	Mon.	Tues.	Wed.	Thurs.	Fri.
# of tantrums	4	2	1	2	1

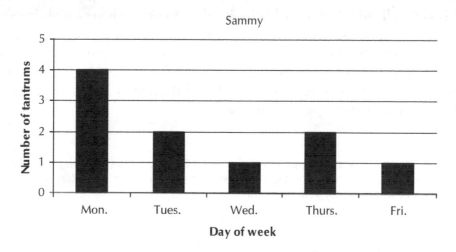

In the above example, keeping a frequency count worked well because Mrs. McIntyre monitored Sammy's behavior over the same period of time each day (8:00–2:30). How would this situation change if Mrs. McIntyre were unable to record Sammy's tantrums for the same amount of time each day? If the observation periods from day to day are not of equal length, Mrs. McIntyre must calculate a ratio of the number of behavioral occurrences in a designated time period (most often number per minute). These calculations are illustrated below:

Day Time	Mon. 8:00–10:00	Tues. 8:30–10:00	Wed. 9:15–9:45	Thurs. 8:00–9:00	Fri. 8:30–9:50
# of tantrums	4	2	1	2	1

Monday's rate = 4 tantrums/2 hours = 2 tantrums per hour

Tuesday's rate = 2 tantrums/1.5 hours = 0.75 tantrums per hour

Wednesday's rate = 1 tantrum/0.5 hours = 2 tantrums per hour

Thursday's rate = 2 tantrums/1 hour = 2 tantrums per hour

FIGURE 4.1. Summarizing frequency data through a bar chart.

found in Appendix 4.1). The entire daily schedule, or even a portion of it, may be incorporated into a scatterplot (see Figure 4.2 for an example). An additional strength of breaking an observation period into intervals, such as through a scatterplot, is that the occurrence of infrequent yet serious behaviors, such as a physical altercation between students, can be captured within days and across weeks.

In summary, the frequency count procedure is appealing given the relative ease with which it can be used. However, the information that is obtained can be limited, and therefore in many situations this information may best be used to complement another procedure. An additional caution regarding the selection of a frequency count procedure is that it is not well suited to record behavior that occurs with very high frequency. For example, if swearing is the behavior of concern, but it is occurring at high rates with instructional periods, attempts to record the behavior may interfere with the presentation of instruction, which may further exacerbate the problem behaviors. Thus the frequency count procedure may best be used for behaviors that occur at low to moderate rates and are relatively discrete and equal in duration.

Mrs. McIntyre could also use a scatterplot to record when Sammy tantrums during the school day. Each time Mrs. McIntyre observes a tantrum, she simply makes a tally mark in the box representing the day and time at which the tantrum occurred.

Student's Name: Sammy   Date/Time: November 3–7

Behavior: tantrums   Setting: classroom

Day					
Time	Mon.	Tues.	Wed.	Thurs.	Fri.
8:00–8:30					
8:30–9:00	III	II		I	IIII
9:00–9:30	recess	recess	recess	recess	recess
9:30–10:00	II	I	II	I	II
10:00–10:30					
10:30–11:00					
11:00–11:30	III	I	II		III
11:30–12:00	lunch	lunch	lunch	lunch	lunch
12:00–12:30					
12:30–1:00	I			II	II
1:00–1:30					
1:30–2:00					
2:00–2:30					
2:30–3:00	I			I	II

After Mrs. McIntyre examines the scatterplot, patterns begin to emerge. Not only does Sammy have more tantrums on Mondays and Fridays, but he also is more likely to have one immediately before and/or after recess and lunch breaks. Knowing this information should be helpful to Mrs. McIntyre in designing appropriate intervention.

FIGURE 4.2. Recording frequency data using a behavioral occurrence scatterplot.

Duration and Latency

A second type of event-based recording involves indicating the length of time of, or prior to, a behavioral occurrence. In duration recording, the length of time over which the behavior occurred is recorded. Some behaviors for which duration recording may be well suited include temper tantrums, studying, thumb sucking, and wandering out of seat. In latency recording, the length of time between a signal and the beginning of a response to the signal is recorded, such as the length of time it takes a student to begin complying with a teacher direction (e.g., how long it takes Susie to line up for lunch following her teacher's direction to the whole class). If completion time for the behavior is needed, duration and latency recording can both be used. Some sort of timing device is most commonly used to record duration and latency data (e.g., stopwatch). As with all event-based techniques, behavioral events must have a clearly defined start and stop point. For example, if a teacher casually tells a student to get ready to go to lunch without specifying to immediately put books away and then get in line, determining when to begin latency recording is difficult.

Data can be summarized by reporting an average or total time, depending on whether length of time relative to another activity (e.g., comparison of response time across instructional activity transitions during a day) or average response (e.g., average response time during transition to lunch) is of interest. As with frequency count recording, collecting concurrent information about setting, antecedent, and consequence events can contextualize the observation data that are obtained. In the previous example, a pattern might be found in the observational data that relates to the nature of the instruction provided by the teacher. A weak nonspecific prompt (e.g., "get ready for lunch") is more likely to be related to a longer latency than a specific prompt (e.g., "get ready for lunch by clearing your desks, and sitting quietly"). If the difference in the antecedent behavior is not noted, the data don't reflect the importance of the quality of the prompt! In summary, duration or latency recording are best used when length of time is of interest, behaviors have clear onset/offset, and conditions under which the behaviors are observed are noted.

Time-Based Recording

A time-based or interval-sampling recording technique is a good choice when (1) behaviors are occurring at high rates or are variable in duration, (2) multiple behaviors or the behaviors of multiple individuals are being recorded, and/or (3) continuous observations are logistically not possible. For example, using a frequency count to record the number of times a student is out-of-seat would not likely be useful if one out of seat event were to last most of an observation period. Examples of school-based behaviors commonly observed using time-based techniques include on/off task, out of seat, looking around, and disruptive behavior.

When using a time-based recording technique, the observation period is divided into prespecified intervals. In applied settings, and depending on who the observer is, each interval is typically set between 15 seconds and 1 to 5 minutes. In general, the smaller the interval, the more behavior can be scored; however, the smaller the interval, the more difficult it can be to conduct the observations. Keeping track of small intervals and teaching at the same time or recording more than one behavior and/or student can be difficult.

Occurrence of target behaviors is recorded (coded) during each interval based on a prespecified rule for when and what to record. Only one code (e.g., + or –, yes or no) is recorded regardless of how many behavioral events occur within an interval. The number of intervals in which the target behavior was observed at least once is divided by the total number of possible observation intervals, and a percentage is calculated. The summary is always percent of intervals in which the behavior was observed (or not) and represents an approximation of the actual number or duration of behavioral occurrences. For example, Amy was observed to be on task during 68% of the observed intervals, Romulus was talking with neighbors for 35% of the observed intervals, and Morgan had his head down and eyes closed during 45% of the observed intervals. It is important to restate that these results are not exact measurements of time or behavioral occurrences; therefore, it is inaccurate to report time-based data as "45% of the time." Time sampling provides an overall *estimate* of behavioral occurrence or nonoccurrence across the specified period. When the size of the observation interval is also factored into the analyses, a potential limitation of time-based observation systems is that they can produce over- or underestimations of the actual behavioral occurrences. This issue is discussed later in the chapter relative to the accuracy of different observation methods.

The behaviors to be observed can be global, such as on-task (coded as +) or off-task (coded as –), or can include multiple codes to provide more specific detail about the behavior occurring. For example, the definition of off-task behavior can be extended to include out of seat (O), looking around (L), calling out (C), and/or talking to peer (T) (descriptions of some of the behaviors most commonly used in observational systems can be found in Table 4.2). Similarly, event- and time-based systems can be combined if a range of behaviors are being recorded. For example, on-task/off-task behavior could be coded using time sampling while simultaneously recording instances (events) of hand raising during each interval. An observer might then report that a student was observed on task for 57% of the observed intervals and raising his hand 7 times or 0.25 times per minute.

Three different time-based techniques (whole interval, partial interval, momentary time sampling) are available for selection depending on what behaviors are being recorded, and when and where observations are being conducted.

Whole Interval

When a whole-interval procedure is used, the behavior is recorded or coded only if it is observed continuously throughout the *entire* or whole interval. For example, if a 30-second whole-interval recording method was being used and Maggie was observed fidgeting during an entire interval, the interval would be scored with a "+." An interval would be recorded with a "–" if (1) she did not start fidgeting until 10 seconds after the beginning of the interval but then fidgeted for the rest of the interval, (2) she was observed fidgeting at the beginning of the interval but stopped 2 seconds before the end of the interval, or (3) she was observed fidgeting at the beginning and end of the interval but was appropriately on task for 5 seconds in the middle of the interval. The accuracy of the scoring can be enhanced by selecting the smallest interval size possible that is logistically manageable for the observer. Whole-interval methods have the potential to underestimate the actual occurrence of the behavior. Thus, whole-interval recording provides a conservative estimate of actual behavior occurrences.

TABLE 4.2. Commonly Observed Behaviors and Associated Definitions

Observation system	Behaviors	Definitions
State–Event Classroom Observation System (SECOS; Saudargas, 1997)	*State behaviors only* Schoolwork	Student has head and eyes oriented toward assigned schoolwork.
	Out of seat	Student is out of his or her seat.
	Looking around	Student is looking around and not engaged in any other activity.
	Motor behavior	Student is engaged in repetitive, stereotyped body movements.
	Play with object	Student is repetitively playing with an object.
	Social interaction with child	Student is interacting with one or more other students.
	Social interaction with teacher	Student is interacting with the classroom teacher.
Behavioral Observation of Students in Schools (BOSS; Shapiro, 1996)	Active engagement	Student is actively and visibly attending to assigned work. Examples include writing, reading aloud, raising hand, discussing responses with peers in a cooperative group.
	Passive engagement	Student is listening to a lecture, looking at an academic worksheet, reading silently, or listening to a peer respond to a question.
	Off-task motor	Student's motor activity is not directly associated with an assignment, such as out-of-seat activity, aimless flipping of pages in a book, drawing, or writing unrelated to the activity.
	Off-task verbal	Student is making audible verbalizations that are not allowed and/or not related to the activity, such as calling out when not asked for a response, forced burping, whistling.
	Passive off-task	Student is not attending to required work (sitting quietly, looking around the room, staring out the window).
Preschool Observation Code (POC; Bramlett, 1993)	*State behaviors only* Play engagement	Student is oriented toward play materials, games, and/or activities.
	Preacademic engagement	Student is oriented toward activities designed to teach specific skills (e.g., numbers, concepts).
	Nonpurposeful play	Student is not engaged in, or is in between, activities.
	Disruptive behaviors	Student is yelling, throwing objects.
	Self-stimulating behaviors	Student is mouthing objects, twirling hair.
	Social interaction—peer	Student is verbally interacting or playing with a peer.
	Teacher monitoring—interacting	Teacher is monitoring activities.

(continued)

TABLE 4.2. (continued)

Observation system	Behaviors	Definitions
Student Observation System (SOS; Reynolds & Kamphaus, 2004b) (Note: The SOS is one component available from the Behavior Assessment System for Children, Second Edition [BASC-2].)	*Adaptive behaviors only*	
	Response to teacher/ lesson	Student is listening to teacher/classmate or following directions, interacting with teacher in class/group, working with teacher one on one, standing at teacher's desk.
	Peer interaction	Student is playing/working with other student(s), talking with other student(s), touching another student appropriately.
	Work on school subjects	Student is doing seatwork, working at blackboard or computer.
	Transition movement	Student is putting on/taking off coat, moving around room (appropriately), preparing materials for beginning/end of lesson, or out of room.
Kehle, Clark, & Jenson (1986)	Disruptive behavior	Student is engaging in behavior involving touching, vocalizing, aggression, playing, disorienting, making noise, and/or out of seat.

Partial Interval

Partial-interval recording differs from whole interval in that the behavior is marked as occurring if it is observed *at any time* during the interval. Using the previous example, if Maggie displayed fidgeting behavior during 3, 10, 20, or 30 seconds of a 30-second interval, a "+" would be scored, indicating that the behavior had occurred. The same score would be provided if within a given interval Maggie fidgeted for 5 seconds, went "on task" for 10 seconds, and then fidgeted again for 4 seconds. Partial-interval recording may be a better choice than whole interval when the behavior is a potentially low-frequency behavior or if observers are not able to observe continuously. In contrast to whole-interval recording, partial-interval recording tends to overestimate the true occurrence of the behavior because behavior is recorded if it occurs during any portion of the interval. Therefore, shorter interval lengths (e.g., 10 seconds) are more desirable and recommended to minimize the overestimation.

Momentary Time Sampling

The third technique, momentary time sampling, is similar to whole and partial interval in that intervals are prespecified. However, recording of behavior occurs only at a specified mark within the interval, typically at the beginning or end. The observer looks at the student and marks the occurrence/nonoccurrence of a behavior only at the end (or beginning) of a specified interval. For example, using a 20-second interval with momentary time sampling, Maggie's fidgeting behavior would be observed during the first second of each new interval and then recorded as occurring or not occurring. This method has two main advantages. First, in contrast to the potential for over- or underestimates of occurrence by other time-sampling methods, research findings have suggested that momentary time sampling may provide a more accurate estimate of true occurrence (see

Saudargas & Lentz, 1986) especially, if the interval size is relatively small (e.g., 20 seconds). A second advantage to momentary time sampling is the simplified nature of simultaneously recording numerous behaviors and/or students and then having sufficient opportunity to record the information between each interval mark. A brief scan of the room at the specified mark can allow the observer to make any and all relevant ratings before the beginning of the next interval. Indeed, some methods capitalize on this advantage to allow for a 20-second period to record frequency count data. In the end, momentary time sampling is an excellent choice when the behavior of interest occurs at a moderate, yet steady rate. In Figure 4.3, a visual comparison of the three time-sampling techniques is provided.

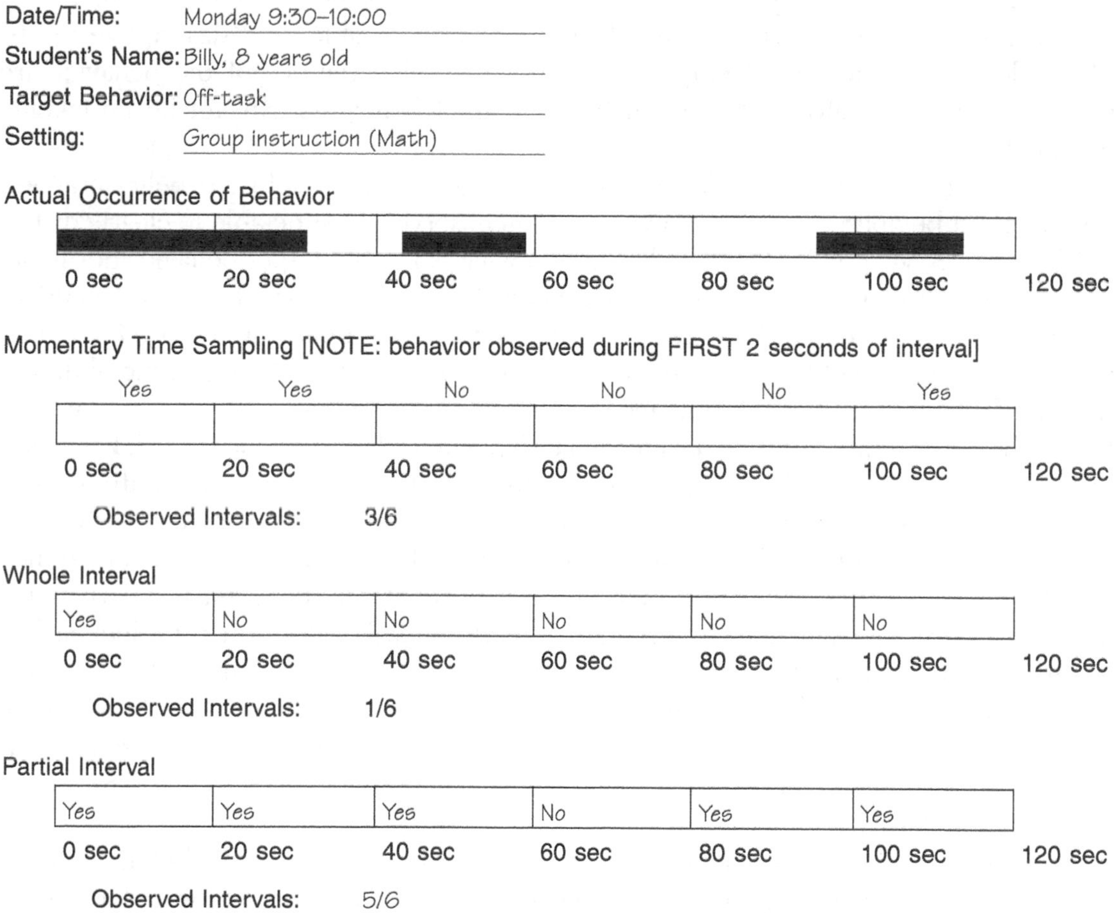

Date/Time: Monday 9:30–10:00

Student's Name: Billy, 8 years old

Target Behavior: Off-task

Setting: Group instruction (Math)

Actual Occurrence of Behavior

| 0 sec | 20 sec | 40 sec | 60 sec | 80 sec | 100 sec | 120 sec |

Momentary Time Sampling [NOTE: behavior observed during FIRST 2 seconds of interval]

| Yes | Yes | No | No | No | Yes |

| 0 sec | 20 sec | 40 sec | 60 sec | 80 sec | 100 sec | 120 sec |

Observed Intervals: 3/6

Whole Interval

| Yes | No | No | No | No | No |

| 0 sec | 20 sec | 40 sec | 60 sec | 80 sec | 100 sec | 120 sec |

Observed Intervals: 1/6

Partial Interval

| Yes | Yes | Yes | No | Yes | Yes |

| 0 sec | 20 sec | 40 sec | 60 sec | 80 sec | 100 sec | 120 sec |

Observed Intervals: 5/6

This example highlights potential discrepancies that may arise when information is collected using each of the available time sampling methods. The first graph indicates that off-task behavior *actually* occurred during approximately half of the observation period. This information is most accurately estimated using momentary time sampling (3/6 intervals), whereas occurrence of off-task behavior is underestimated if only whole intervals are recorded (1/6 intervals) and overestimated if partial intervals are recorded (5/6 intervals).

FIGURE 4.3. Comparison of momentary time sampling, whole-interval, and partial-interval recording using a 20-second interval.

HOW DO YOU SELECT AND DEFINE BEHAVIORS
TO BE OBSERVED DURING SDO?

As previously noted, the goal of SDO is to quantify behavior. The target behavior to be quantified can vary depending on the specific situation. However, the first consideration is to define the specific behaviors in observable/measurable terms—that is, to answer the question "What behaviors am I interested in and what outcome data do I need?" Consideration should be given to narrowing and defining. Narrowing refers to selecting the smallest number of behaviors that are of particular interest or that answer a specific question. Although trying to monitor a long list of behaviors is tempting, the longer the list, the more difficult looking for, evaluating, and recording the behaviors become. A general guideline is to limit the list to two or three significant behaviors, and monitor those behaviors with integrity. After the number of behaviors to be observed has been narrowed, each behavior must be defined in specific, observable, and descriptive terms. These definitions must be "comprehensive" in that all variations of the behavior are included, and "mutually exclusive" in that nontarget behaviors can not be mistakenly included.

To ensure that definitions are comprehensive and mutually exclusive, behavioral definitions must be operational in nature, that is, an observer must be able to clearly distinguish between what is the target behavior and what is not the target behavior during an observation. Similarly, a good operational definition is one in which two independent observers could agree that they saw or did not see the target behavior because the topography or appearance of the behavior is specific and observable. Although general definitions might be interpreted as being good because they would "catch" more behavior, they tend to be make it difficult to determine what should and should not be scored. For example, if the behavior is called "aggression" without further specification, confusion can result about whether to include verbal and physical forms as well as aggressive acts toward persons and objects. As another example, even though "on task" has been defined as "student is oriented toward the teacher and/or is actively engaged in instructional activities," observers may question whether to mark "on task" if the student is looking at a teacher who is speaking but not acknowledging questions, or if it is difficult to see what the student is writing, or if the student displays a hand raise in response to a teacher question but is looking out the window. In all of these examples, behavioral definitions need to be narrowed, and multiple examples and nonexamples are needed to ensure agreement about what to score.

Examples of behaviors and possible associated definitions are provided in Table 4.2 to illustrate how behaviors might be selected and defined. The examples were taken from a range of SDO publications used for practice and research purposes. When selecting and defining the behavior(s) of interest, some further considerations are in order. First, the observation setting should guide behavior selection. The behaviors and definitions included in Table 4.2 are common to classroom-based settings. Similar and different behaviors and definitions would be reflected for other settings, for example, playground, bus, hallway, and home. In addition, developmental considerations in behavior selection may be in order. For example, although similar in intent to other behaviors listed in the table, the behaviors indicated under the Preschool Observation Code (Bramlett, 1993) were modified to be more age appropriate for a preschool population.

When concerned with a particular clinical population, such as students with attention-deficit/hyperactivity disorder (ADHD), common clinical descriptors and definitions should be considered. For example, the Attention Deficit Hyperactivity Disorder School Observation Code (ADHDSOC; Gadow, Sprafkin, & Nolan, 1996) involves behavioral categories for both classroom and lunchroom/playground settings. The class-based observations include interference, motor movement, noncompliance, verbal aggression, symbolic aggression, object aggression, and off task. Lunchroom and playground behaviors include appropriate social behavior, noncompliance, nonphysical aggression, verbal aggression, and physical aggression.

Finally, observing interactions between the target student and others (such as the teacher and/or parent) may be an important piece in obtaining a complete picture of the context surrounding behavior. In these instances, clear definitions for the behaviors of the student and the other target individuals would be important. A few example behaviors for teacher observation are included in Table 4.2. Merrell (2003) provided a review of useful observation systems for home- or clinic-based settings, including observation of behavior such as child noncompliance during parent interactions and aversive family behavior.

HOW DO YOU CHOOSE A SYSTEM FOR COLLECTING SDO DATA?

Selecting a system for collecting SDO data begins with determining the behaviors of interest and an appropriate type of data-recording method. Once these decisions have been made, the next step is to create a paper-and-pencil method for recording the data. For example, to record frequency data, basic background information (e.g., student name, date, activity, observer) is noted at the top of the paper, and tally marks are made for each observed occurrence of behavior. A more elaborate way to collect frequency data across an entire day could be through the use of a scatterplot (see Appendix 4.1). Time or activity could be indicated on the left-hand column as a way to represent the entire school day. In Appendix 4.2, a sample form for recording on-task/off-task behavior is provided, whereas the form in Appendix 4.3 includes space to select and define other behaviors. Procedures for using each of the time-sampling techniques are included on the sample forms.

An alternative to creating your own observation forms is to use an existing, published system. Again, the appropriateness of a particular system depends in large part on the behaviors of interest. A summary of several existing systems for recording school-based behavior is given in Table 4.3. The State–Event Classroom Observation System (SECOS; Saudargas, 1997), the Behavioral Observation of Students in Schools (BOSS; Shapiro, 1996), and the Student Observation System (SOS; Reynolds & Kamphaus, 2004b) are well known and frequently used in the observation of behaviors common to classroom settings. In addition, examples of measures that allow the observer to target more specific situations and/or behaviors are included. Although classroom settings present a good opportunity for observation of student behavior, Leff and Lakin (2005) indicate that other, unstructured settings, such as the playground, offer an important context for a full understanding of a child's behavior (e.g., peer relationships, play behaviors, and aggressive actions). Two examples from their review of playground or play-based observation systems also are included.

TABLE 4.3. Some Examples of Existing Systems for Conducting Systematic Direct Observation in School Settings

Observation system	Brief description	Recording system
State–Event Classroom Observation System (SECOS; Saudargas, 1997)	Allows simultaneous observation of multiple classroom-relevant behaviors. Also provides opportunity to code interactions with teacher.	Momentary time sampling for state behaviors, frequency count for event behaviors.
Behavioral Observation of Students in Schools (BOSS; Shapiro, 1996)	Emphasis on academic behavior in the classroom, particularly engagement (passive and active). Also allows for peer comparison and estimation of amount of time teacher engaged in direct instruction.	Momentary time sampling for engagement, partial-interval time sampling for off-task behaviors.
Student Observation System (SOS; Reynolds & Kamphaus, 2004) (*Note*: The SOS is one component available from the Behavior Assessment System for Children, Second Edition [BASC-2], available from AGS Publishing [*www.agsnet.com*].)	Appropriate for observing adaptive and maladaptive classroom behavior of children in preschool through high school. In addition to paper-and-pencil version, available for use on computer or PDA.	Momentary time sampling. Also includes sections for narrative comments of teacher–student interaction and observer's overall rating of behaviors observed.
Attention Deficit Hyperactivity Disorder School Observation Code (Gadow, Sprafkin, & Nolan, 1996)	Described as useful for screening and evaluating ADHD intervention effects across multiple school settings (e.g., classroom, lunchroom, playground). Target behaviors emphasized include disruptive and aggressive areas. Peer comparison recommended.	Partial-interval time sampling.
Peer Social Behavior of the Systematic Screening for Behavior Disorders (PSB of the SSBD; Walker & Severson, 1991)	The PSB component offers a playground-based observation system for use in the final stage of the SSBD, a screening process to identify children at risk for serious behavioral disorders. Target behaviors include social engagement, parallel play, alone, and not codable.	Partial-interval time sampling.
Preschool Observation Code (POC; Bramlett, 1993)	Similar to the SECOS but behaviors included are modified for preschool ages.	Momentary time sampling for state behaviors, frequency counts for event behaviors.

The ADHDSOC (Gadow et al., 1996), mentioned previously, is a well-established measure with particular applications for children who display significant externalizing behaviors. It is described as straightforward and easy to learn. The Peer Social Behavior of the Systematic Screening for Behavior Disorders (PSB of the SSBD; Walker & Severson, 1991) is another established system with an impressive record of use across several large-scale studies. The PSB is a playground-based observation system that serves as one piece of the SSBD three-stage screening process for children at risk for serious behavioral disorders. Although described as a highly acceptable and cost-efficient system, the PSB is primarily considered to be a screening tool and is typically used in conjunction with the entire SSBD process. A final example presented in Table 4.3 is a code appropriate for use in the observation of preschool children, the Preschool Observation Code (POC; Bramlett, 1993).

Another possibility for selecting a system can be found in a growing number of computer-based applications that can be used on a laptop and/or personal digital assistant (i.e., handheld). For example, a new software application has been released as part of the Behavior Assessment System for Children (BASC-2; Reynolds & Kamphaus, 2004). Using the BASC-2 Portable Observation Program, a computer or PDA can be used to conduct direct observation of multiple behaviors and/or students. The observation templates can be customized or the BASC-2 Student Observation System template can be specified. The authors anecdotally report that training takes less than 1 hour. Multiple observation reports may be saved and printed in PDF or RTF files. !Observe (Martin, 2001) is another software application that can be used with a personal digital assistant (PDA) and/or a computer by observers interested in collecting behavioral data for up to 24 different behaviors using either event or interval recording. Preconfigured observation templates are also available. Graphs and tables are easily generated, and data can be exported to word-processing or spreadsheet programs. Another example of a PDA software package for observing behavior is the Comprehensive Behavior Tracking System (Oswald, 2000), which is designed to allow observers to gather data on multiple behaviors and/or students using user-determined intervals (time sampling). In addition, event recording can be conducted. Data files can be edited within the PDA or transferred to spreadsheet or text file programs on a personal computer. A final example certainly worth mentioning is Ecobehavioral Assessment Software Systems (EBASS Version 3; Greenwood, Carta, Kamps, Terry, & Delquadri, 1994), which was developed at Juniper Gardens Children's Project (*www.jgcp.ku.edu*). The EBASS is a comprehensive computer software system involving separate instruments. These instruments include the Ecobehavioral System for Complex Assessments of Preschool Environments (ESCAPE), Code for Instructional Structure and Student Academic Response (CISSAR), and the mainstream version of CISSAR (MS-CISSAR). The instruments can be used to observe and analyze the behavior of individual students and classroom situations (ecology and teacher) and can also be used to generate hypotheses for use in functional analysis. Although impressive, comprehensive, and likely to be of great value to school psychologists, the EBASS can be costly and is considered complex, thus requiring intensive training in order to become fluent in its use. Given the relatively new introduction of software packages for recording data and an ever-changing field of technology, Dumont and Chafouleas (1999) recommend careful review of what a program can do in relation to your needs. For example, efficiency is often touted as a reason for using technology. Although the relative effectiveness and efficiency of software programs over paper-and-pencil methods have not been demonstrated yet, advances in the technology are likely to expand the accuracy and usefulness of SDO methods.

HOW DO YOU SUMMARIZE DATA COLLECTED FROM SDO?

A significant advantage of using SDO over other direct observation techniques is the ability to analyze and present information in useful ways. Specifically, multiple data points can be quantified, compared, combined, and summarized to be used in both summative and formative purposes. For example, weeklong recording of the frequency of

Sammy's tantrum behavior can be summarized into a statement of total occurrence (10 per week), average daily occurrence (2 per day), most likely time of occurrence (morning after math instruction), and so on. In addition, and perhaps more importantly, Sammy's tantrum behavior before an intervention was implemented can be compared to data collected after the intervention starts. This opportunity to compare across two conditions allows for an understanding of the impact of an intervention on a target behavior. In each of these examples, a standardized observation method is required.

Options for summarizing data depend on the type of data recording system. As in Sammy's example above, event data can be tallied and organized as desired and then may be presented in a visual format using a bar or line graph. (See Figure 4.1 for an example of a bar chart.) Generally, these data from time-based recording systems are presented as a percentage of observed intervals in which the behavior of interest was or was not observed. Because time-based methods (unlike event-based methods) involve determination of the presence or absence of behavior within an interval, they result in approximations of the actual occurrence of behavioral events (indirect). Thus, results are reported as "behavior was observed to occur in X percentage of intervals" rather than "behavior was observed to occur X percentage of the time." As with event based methods, data can then be summarized and graphed as appropriate (e.g., bar or line graphs). Typically, the y axis would be labeled with what is being described (e.g., "% of observed intervals"), and the x axis would be labeled with time (e.g., session, day). An example is provided in Figure 4.4. When deciding how much data should be collected to represent actual student behavior, a general rule of thumb is to have at least three stable data points. If data are highly variable, evaluation of results is difficult, particularly when making decisions about intervention effectiveness.

WHAT ARE THE STRENGTHS ASSOCIATED WITH SDO TECHNIQUES?

Directness

The power of SDO is direct observation of behavioral occurrences by an observer/recorder. In contrast, when raters are asked to retrospectively assess behavior (e.g., behavior rating scales), accuracy can be affected by time, memory, intervening experiences, etc. Thus, the closer in time that behavior is recorded to actual occurrence, the greater the potential for more objective data, especially if definitions and procedures are clearly described. Objective data require lower inference and fewer steps to interpretation.

Flexibility

Another highly attractive feature of SDO is the ability to tailor SDO methods to fit individual situations. Although some examples of established observation systems are designed to target specific behaviors (e.g., ADHDSOC), less specialized direct observation methods can be used to monitor virtually any behavior from off-task to aggressive behavior. Basically, you can use SDO to record any behavior that is observable, has a discrete beginning and end, and is operationally defined. Furthermore, depending on the complexity of the observation system, SDO procedures can be used to monitor the behavior(s) of an individual or a group of individuals simultaneously.

Ms. Kaufman, the school psychologist, has been asked to observe Sara's behavior during independent work time. Sara's teacher is concerned that she spends a significant amount of class time staring out the window and doodling instead of working on her assignments. Ms. Kaufman agrees to observe Sara over the next week. During these observation periods, she will utilize a momentary time sampling procedure (15-second intervals) to record the percentage of intervals in which she observes Sara engaging in on-task behavior (defined as "Sara is oriented toward the teacher and/or is actively engaged in instructional activities"). Ms. Kaufman also plans to collect the same data for a same-sex peer in order to examine Sara's behavior in comparison to her classmates. Ms. Kaufman's data are provided below:

Subject	Sara			Peer (comparison)		
	Number of on-task intervals	Total number of intervals	Percentage of on-task intervals	Number of on-task intervals	Total number of intervals	Percentage of on-task intervals
Day 1	18	40	45	28	40	70
Day 2	21	60	35	51	60	85
Day 3	44	80	55	72	80	90
Day 4	24	60	40	51	60	85
Day 5	39	60	65	57	60	95

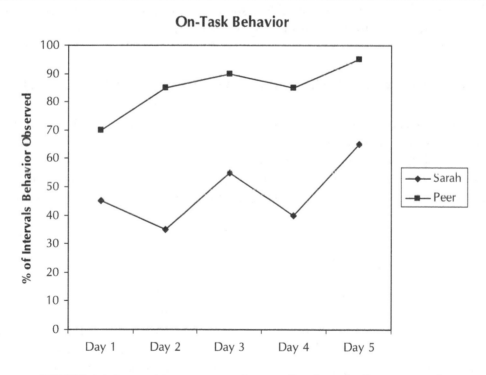

On-Task Behavior

FIGURE 4.4. Summarizing momentary time sampling through a line series graph.

Usefulness in Progress Monitoring

Unlike behavior rating scales, which provide a global assessment of behavior over a longer period, SDO allows for continuous measurement—which is needed in progress monitoring. For example, use of a momentary time-sampling technique may reveal that disruptive behavior occurred in 30–50% of observed intervals before some intervention, and in 0–15% of observed intervals postintervention. Such information is critical in the analysis of behavior change over time. Because the range of measurement is not limited, changes in behavior that occur from one observation to the next are easier to detect.

Standardized Procedures

Another advantage of using SDO for collecting and summarizing behavioral data is that standardized procedures allow for reliable comparisons across observation sessions. Comparisons can be made across other dimensions as well (e.g., rater, students, settings).

Minimal Cost for Materials

Direct observation can be relatively cost free or inexpensive with regard to material resources. For individuals using a paper-based method of recording, the cost could be limited to photocopies and writing utensils. As use of technology increases, however, so do costs related to hardware, software, and technical assistance and maintenance. Decisions to invest in more expensive data recording and storing methods and equipment should be guided by other cost variables, such as time, intrusiveness, ease, and steps/manipulations required to go from raw to summary data.

WHAT WEAKNESSES ARE ASSOCIATED WITH SDO TECHNIQUES?

Although the advantages of using SDO are clear, the procedures are not without flaws. As reviewed by Merrell (2003), even strong advocates of direct observation would concede the existence of various threats to the data. Without careful attention to potential sources of influence, reliability and validity of the obtained data can become questionable. Thus, we provide an overview of various sources of influence and discuss ways to reduce the effects of each one.

Difficulty with Definition Specificity

An important first consideration when using SDO relates to the target behavior itself and the associated coding system. How well and specifically a target behavior has been defined affects how well the definition can be applied to a given behavioral event. For example, a more global target behavior, such as "on task," requires greater inference when deciding how to code the behavior "raising hand." For example, use of the term "disruptive behavior" is appropriate only if the acceptable variations of this behavior are completely explained. Although most of us would not tend to equate "belching" with "throwing chairs," both can be considered disruptive and each may be important to record.

Practically speaking, using event recording to note instances of "hand raising" may require less inference than recording instances of "out of seat" behavior displayed by the child who frequently moves around the vicinity of her seat (picture a backside "hovering" 4 inches above and next to the actual seat!). On the other hand, defining a behavior with too much specificity (e.g., 10 different subcategories of "on-task" behavior) may make recording too cumbersome, and, as a result, data obtained may be too narrow to be important in understanding the full picture of student behavior. In addition, such extreme specificity can narrow the behavior to the point of irrelevance, or errors could occur because of the added complexity associated with collecting data on a large number of behaviors. In the end, the goal is to establish a careful balance between being too specific and too global when operationally defining behaviors to be observed and recorded.

Reactivity

SDO generally requires the presence of an external observer within a natural setting (e.g., classroom, playground). Unfortunately, a target child (or teacher) who knows that he or she is being observed often may react by changing behavior and thereby decreasing the representiveness of the observation. This phenomenon, known as *reactivity*, affects not only the behaviors of the target student and teacher but also the whole class as other children notice a rater sitting in the room. Signs of student reactivity include, for example, staring, waving, or directing questions at the observer.

[handwritten margin note: can affect data validity]

In a related manner, changes in the representiveness of the "typical" class (e.g., large number of new students or visitors, high number of absences, substitute teacher) can affect typical behavioral occurrences. Options for limiting potential reactivity include entering the setting at a natural transition point, avoiding use of equipment that may attract attention, and familiarizing yourself with the classroom prior to official observation to allow students to adjust to observer presence (Merrell, 2003). Regardless, the rater must remember that teachers may be correct when they say "the class was totally different with you in the room."

Observer Error and Observer Drift

Whenever humans are involved in scoring or measurement, the potential for error exists. A first general concern relates to who scores or codes the data. Observers differ in their personal characteristics, previous knowledge and expectations about the child or situation, experience with the technique, and so on. (For a complete review of possible sources of personal error, see Sattler, 2002, p. 132.) One important source of observer error is called "observer drift," which occurs when observers deviate from the original definitions of behavior and change their recording habits. Observer drift can be associated with fatigue, forgetfulness, decreased motivation, or loss of interest. The potential for observer drift can be limited through careful attention to high-quality initial training in the observation system as well as periodic retraining. Although this is often overlooked, even experienced educational professionals need periodic skill tune-ups. In addition, reliability checks, such as through calculation of interobserver agreement, may be important in alerting the observer to potential influences in the data.

One simple formula for calculating an approximate interobserver agreement when using time sampling data (interval) involves dividing the number of agreements by the number of agreements plus the number of disagreements, multiplied by 100. An example demonstrating use of this procedure is presented in Figure 4.5. Calculating agreement for event-based data involves dividing the smaller number of behavioral occurrences reported by one observer with the larger number of behavioral occurrences by the other observer and multiplying by 100. According to Sattler (2002), percent agreement that falls at 80% or above is considered satisfactory.

For a more precise determination of interscorer agreement, one might want to calculate "kappa." Kappa measures the degree of consensus among multiple observers and can be used when data are on an ordinal scale and interest is in correcting for chance agreement (see Figure 4.5 for an example of how to calculate kappa with two observers). Various computer programs can be used to calculate kappa (see Sattler, 2002, pp. 135–137). MacKappa (Watkins, 1998) is an example of a computer program for calculating kappa coefficients (downloadable free of charge from *espse.ed.psu.edu/Spsy/Watkins/Watkins3.ssi*). In summary, whether during initial training or retraining, observers must understand thoroughly the definition of the target behavior and the system for recording behavior and data collection must be monitored to ensure adequate reliability.

Interval	1	2	3	4	5	6	7	8	9	10
Observer 1	+	–	+	+	+	–	–	+	+	+
Observer 2	+	+	+	+	+	–	–	+	+	–
Agreement?	Y	N	Y	Y	Y	Y	Y	Y	Y	N

Formula: % Agreement = [Number of Agreements/(Number of Agreements plus Disagreements)] × 100

% Agreement = [8/(8 + 2)] × 100

% Agreement = 80%

	Observer 1 Behavior Present	Observer 1 Behavior Absent	
Observer 2 Behavior Present	6	1	7
Observer 2 Behavior Absent	1	2	3
	7	3	10

Kappa = $(P_O - P_C)/(1 - P_C)$

P_O (percent agreement) = agreements/(agreements + disagreements)

P_C (chance agreement) = $[(X_1 \times Y_1)/N^2] + [(X_r \times Y_r)/N^2]$

P_O = 8/(8 + 2) = 8/10 = .80

P_C = $[(7 \times 7)/10^2] + [(3 \times 3)/10^2]$ = (49/100) + (9/100) = .58

Kappa = (.80 – .58)/(1 – .58) = .22/.42 = .52

FIGURE 4.5. Calculating percent agreement and kappa. Kappa example adapted from Watkins and Pacheco (2000).

Limited Feasibility in Terms of Training and Intrusiveness

Using SDO in applied settings can have limited feasibility. Individual observation sessions may not seem overly burdensome, as they may only last 15 or 20 minutes; however, rarely would a single observation be considered appropriately representative of student behavior. Most situations require repeated observations over time. The time required to collect data can quickly add up, particularly if the time required for summarizing and interpreting your data are considered. In addition, SDO usually requires the presence of an external observer when it is difficult for the classroom teacher to instruct the whole class and collect data on a particular individual at the same time. Depending on the staffing resources in a given school, finding sufficient personnel to conduct needed observation sessions also can be difficult. As a result, SDO methods might be reserved for high-stakes situations in environments with limited staffing resources.

Difficulty Monitoring Low-Frequency Behaviors

Problem behaviors that occur infrequently and/or inconsistently may be difficult to monitor using SDO. For example, if Michael has been referred for demonstrating "aggressive outbursts," but this behavior only occurs once or twice per month, it may be difficult for an outside observer to schedule an appropriate observation session. If Michael typically has these outbursts right before lunch, scheduling would be less of a problem. On the other hand, when no apparent pattern to his outbursts exists, the probability of the behavior occurring during the observation session will be low to zero. Rather than depending on an external observer, data collection might be conducted, for example, by existing classroom personnel (e.g., classroom teacher, aide).

Generalizability

Given that each observation session typically occurs for a relatively short period of time (e.g., 15–30 minutes), the behaviors observed may not be representative of what occurs throughout the typical school day. For example, if Mr. Jones conducts SDO during math instruction and finds that Nick was off task during 55% of intervals, Mr. Jones cannot assume that Nick would exhibit similar rates of off-task behavior during reading instruction or even during independent math seatwork. SDO only provides information about behavior at a specific point in time and under specific setting or environmental conditions. Repeated measures within and across different settings can increase the representiveness of observed and reported data.

Hintze and Matthews (2004) suggest that "accuracy" be defined as the extent to which the observed score represents the true score (Cone, 1977) and "interobserver agreement" refers to the degree of association between data collected concurrently by two observers (Kazdin, 1982). The reliability of direct observation of on-task/off-task behavior may be improved through the use of generalizability (G) theory (for a review of G theory, see Hintze & Matthews, 2004). Hintze and Matthews (2004) found that despite adequate levels of interobserver agreement, adequate levels of reliability across time and setting could not be obtained even with observation two times per day over 2 weeks—

which certainly seems extensive to the school-based practitioner! Thus, the main messages are that reliability improves with repeated observation, and that these data should not be used to make generalized statements about a student's behavior. Any statement should be clearly linked to the time and environment in which the measurement occurred.

CONCLUDING COMMENTS

In this chapter, we have described several techniques for conducting systematic observation. In particular, guidelines were provided for determining which recording techniques are appropriate for which types of behaviors. The questions that need to be answered to guide systematic observation are why data are being collected, how to define a behavior, what data to collect, and which recording technique should be used. However, the process always begins with understanding what questions need to be answered. In summary, regardless of the specific SDO technique selected, the following guidelines apply when using SDO:

1. Specify the question or problem that needs to be answered.
2. Define the behavior in observable terms, that is, topography (appearance), beginning/end, typical duration, and so forth.
3. Identify and describe times when and places where the behaviors are most and least likely to occur.
4. Determine whether an event- or time-based system is most appropriate given the behaviors and the setting.
5. If possible, record proximal setting, antecedent, and consequence events that relate to behavioral occurrences.
6. Implement the observation system consistently in the same time and location.
7. Check for accuracy of data recording on a regular basis.
8. Summarize data in terms that answer the initial question or problem.

BEHAVIORAL OCCURRENCE SCATTERPLOT

DIRECTIONS: This graph can be used to record event behaviors (when interested in simply recording occurrence or nonoccurrence of a behavior). List the days of the week across the first row (e.g., Mon., Tues., Wed.) and times or activities down the first column (e.g., 9:00–9:15, Spelling lesson). When a target behavior occurs, place an X in the box that corresponds with the appropriate date and time. After completing the chart, look for any patterns that emerge (i.e., are most of the X's clustered in the morning? before recess or lunch?).

Student's Name: _____   Date/Time: _____

Behavior: _____   Setting: _____

Day

Time										

Comments:

TIME-SAMPLING RECORDING FORM
FOR ON-TASK/OFF-TASK BEHAVIOR

Student: _____   Date/Time: _____

Teacher: _____   Observer: _____

Observation Activity: _____

DIRECTIONS: Momentary time-sampling procedures are used to code on-task (+) or off-task (-) behavior. Using a stopwatch, observe target student (white boxes) and a same-sex peer (shaded boxes) and record the observed behavior *at the beginning* of each 20-second interval. (Record target student observation data first.) Compute the percentage of intervals of on-task or off-task behavior by calculating the number of +'s divided by 30 and multiplying by 100 [(+'s/30) × 100].

Interval	Target	Peer		Interval	Target	Peer		Interval	Target	Peer
1				11				21		
2				12				22		
3				13				23		
4				14				24		
5				15				25		
6				16				26		
7				17				27		
8				18				28		
9				19				29		
10				20				30		

Percentage on-task behavior:

COMBINED-TECHNIQUE OBSERVATION RECORDING FORM

Target Student's Name _____   Date: _____

Teacher: _____   Time: _____

Observation Activity: _____

Observer's Name: _____

DIRECTIONS: This form can be used to code two behaviors during the same observation period for both the target student and a same-sex peer. The first two columns should be used to record any behaviors that do not have a clear beginning and/or end using a time-sampling technique (e.g., momentary time sampling). The second two columns should be used to record discrete behaviors using an event-based technique (e.g., frequency count). Record the target student's behavior first.

Time-based behavior: _____

Operational definition of behavior: _____

_____

Event-based behavior: _____

Operational definition of behavior: _____

	Time-Based		Event-Based				Time-Based		Event-Based	
	T	P	T	P			T	P	T	P
1						21				
2						22				
3						23				
4						24				
5						25				
6						26				
7						27				
8						28				
9						29				
10						30				
11						31				
12						32				
13						33				
14						34				
15						35				
16						36				
17						37				
18						38				
19						39				
20						40				

5

Direct Behavior Ratings

In this chapter, the use of direct behavior ratings (DBRs) in behavioral assessment is reviewed. Guidelines are provided for determining the appropriateness of using the DBR along with suggestions for designing and implementing it.

WHAT ARE DBRs AND WHY USE THEM?

Direct behavior ratings refer to a category of hybrid assessment tools that combine characteristics of systematic direct observation (SDO) and behavior rating scales. Like systematic direct observation, these tools are designed to be used in a formative (repeated) fashion to represent behavior that occurs over a specified period of time (e.g., 4 weeks) and under specific and similar conditions (e.g., 45-minute morning independent seatwork). However, as with behavior rating scales, using these tools requires rating target behavior on a scale, such as rating the degree to which Johnny was actively engaged. So, teachers might be asked to rate on a scale from 1 (not at all) to 10 (almost always) the degree to which Johnny was actively engaged in work activities during independent seatwork this morning. Thus, although the rating process may be similar to that for a traditional behavior rating scale, the DBR tagrets a specified shorter period of time, making it a more direct behavior assessment tool. As a result, DBRs can be useful in progress monitoring given the potential efficiency with which the rating can be completed. We elaborate on these points later, but first discuss the characteristics of the DBR.

Although we use the term DBR to describe this category of assessment tools, the DBR is not necessarily a new tool. Other terms have been used to describe it. For example, terms such as Home–School Note, Behavior Report Card, Daily Progress Report, and Good Behavior Note may be more widely recognized in school settings. Within the literature, Steege, Davin, and Hathaway (2001) referred to this assessment technique as a performance-based behavioral recording. Chafouleas, Riley-Tillman, and McDougal (2002) discussed this technique as a Daily Behavior Report Card (DBRC). They noted that when a DBRC is used, a behavior is specified and rating of that behavior occurs over a defined period of time. The obtained information is then shared across individuals (e.g., teacher to parent, teacher to student) and can be used to monitor the effects of an intervention (i.e., as an assessment tool) and/or as a component of an intervention (e.g., self-monitoring). Although the term may vary within the literature and in practice, we believe the DBR descriptor captures the essential characteristics of the tool, that is, a brief rating of target behavior over a specified period of time.

The broad definition of a DBR provides flexibility to design the actual rating and procedures based on the situation. As summarized by Chafouleas and colleagues (2002), DBRs can vary according to the behavior to be rated (e.g., academic or social, increase or decrease in target behavior); type of rating system (e.g., checklist, scale); rating frequency (e.g., once daily, throughout the day, once weekly); rater (e.g., child, teacher); target of rating (e.g., individual, classwide); frequency with which information is shared with another person (e.g., daily, weekly); consequence utilized (e.g., positive, negative); and setting for delivery of the consequence (e.g., home, school, other) (see Table 5.1). The kinds of decisions that are made will depend on the behavior of interest as well as the context or situation of concern.

This broad definition of a DBR allows a similar form of assessment tool to be used across different types of classrooms and schools. That is, the customizable nature of the DBR makes it applicable for use across school settings, grades, behaviors of interest, and so on. For example, in a recent survey of teachers across disciplines and grades, approximately two thirds indicated favorable acceptability and use of a tool like the DBR for different reasons, including assessment, communication, and intervention (Chafouleas, Riley-Tillman, & Sassu, 2006). However, using DBR data in assessment requires some important clarifications. For the purposes of this chapter, the term DBR will refer to a "systematic DBR" based on criteria similar to those used to distinguish naturalistic observation from systematic direct observation (see Chapter 4; Salvia & Ysseldyke, 2004;

TABLE 5.1. Guiding Questions When Designing the DBR

What is the target behavior and goal?
- Focus on a specific behavior (e.g., calling out) or a cluster term for behaviors (e.g., disruption)
- Goal to increase or decrease behavior

Who is the focus of the rating?
- Individual, small-group, or classwide

What is the period for rating?
- Specific school period, daily, or other

What is the setting of observation?
- Classroom or other location

How often will data be collected?
- Multiple times a day, daily, weekly

What scale for rating will be used?
- Checklist, Likert-type scale, continuous line

Who will conduct the rating?
- Classroom teacher, aide, or other educational professional

Will ratings be tied to consequences?
- Consequences must be consistently delivered by person responsible

Hintze & Matthews, 2004). Applying these criteria to the DBR, a systematic DBR possesses the following four characteristics:

1. The behavior of interest must be operationally defined.
2. The observations should be conducted using standardized procedures.
3. The DBR should be used at a specific time and place, and at a predetermined frequency.
4. The data must be scored and summarized in a consistent manner.

These criteria are consistent with those presented for direct observation and are important because DBRs are already accepted and used in schools. Thus it should not be expected that all DBR data can be appropriately used for assessment purposes. For example, when the DBR is not used "systematically," the obtained data may not be useful in monitoring behavior due to an inability to compare information across time or settings. In addition, data may be interpreted differently by various consumers given the lack of standardization. Having a standardized methodology allows for multiple persons in the classroom to rate a child on the same behaviors using consistent procedures. For example, a classroom teacher and an aide could both collect DBR data on the aggressive behavior of a student, and the reliability of those data across raters could be examined. Another reason to follow these criteria is that available research to date is based on the use of systematic DBRs. As a result, all of the strengths and weaknesses discussed with regard to DBRs are based on the assumption that DBRs are standardized, and thus it would be inaccurate to generalize findings to all forms of DBR. Simply put, to use a DBR in a reliable and valid fashion, it must meet the relevant criteria for a "systematic" DBR.

WHEN SHOULD DBRs BE USED?

In determining the appropriateness of using a DBR, we reconsider our guiding questions:

1. Why do you need the data?
2. Which tools are the best match to assess the behavior of interest?
3. What decisions will be made using the data?
4. What resources are available to collect the data?

In general, DBRs appear to be an effective and efficient option in low-priority situations when multiple data are needed on the same student(s) and/or behavior(s), when resources are limited, and when educators are willing to use the DBR. The utility of DBR may be limited because of two issues.

First, an extensive empirical base supporting the accuracy and reliability of DBR data does not yet exist. Although results should be considered preliminary, one recent line of research has focused on the technical characteristics of DBR, which are important in understanding the types of decisions that can be made using DBR data. These initial studies compare reliability and accuracy of DBR to systematic direct observation. In one study, researchers determined that a DBR (i.e., performance-based behavioral recording procedure) was reliable and accurate for recording the specified behaviors exhibited by persons with developmental disabilities (Steege et al., 2001). That is, trends in ratings of the behaviors over time were similar between the DBR and direct observation data. Likewise, Chafouleas, McDougal, Riley-Tillman, Panahon, and Hilt (2005) compared information obtained from DBR and systematic direct observation across different raters and found a significant positive correlation between systematic direct observation data collected by an outside observer and DBR data collected by a classroom teacher. This study was then replicated to further support the correlation between DBR and systematic direct observation data (Riley-Tillman, Chafouleas, Sassu, Chanese, & Glazer, 2006). Together, these studies provide initial support for the DBR as a potentially feasible supplement to systematic direct observation. However, future research must specifically examine sensitivity to change in order to better understand the capacity of the DBR for use in progress monitoring purposes.

Another relevant issue is that, by definition, data obtained from a DBR are comprised of the rater's perception of the child's behavior. As a result, when high-stakes decisions are to be made (e.g., out-of-school placement), reliance on DBR data alone is risky given that we do not yet fully understand the impact of raters on the data. For example, recent work has suggested that although similar overall DBR profiles may be obtained across raters, data points will not be exactly the same from rater to rater (see Chafouleas, Christ, Riley-Tillman, Briesch, & Chanese, 2007; Chafouleas, Riley-Tillman, Sassu, LaFrance, & Patwa, 2007). These findings suggest that when a DBR is used, the same rater should be used across all ratings. For example, in his work on teacher perceptions of the ideal student, H. Walker (personal communication, June 20, 2006) has found that teachers universally endorse a similar profile of attributes, yet differ significantly in their tolerance levels for deviant behavior. Thus, further research is needed to understand the influence of raters on DBR data, and as with most high-stakes decisions, a sole source of data is probably not adequate. Additionally, DBR data are best used in intraindividual rather than interindividual comparison, such as in diagnostic or progress monitoring assessment.

Despite the limited empirical attention to date, a DBR may be a good choice in many situations because completing it is quick and easy with respect to resources and effort. For example, we might want to answer the following questions: "Is a classwide intervention effective for changing a particular student's problematic behavior?" or "Does a child continue to display inappropriate calling-out behavior when reading material at his instructional level is provided?" In the ideal situation, we would recommend the frequent collection of behavioral observation data; however, in applied settings, resources and time are far too limited to support this intensive form of information collection. Thus, when making "lower-stakes" decisions, the DBR may be a good fit. For example, Mr. Cohen is the sole school psychologist in Sunnyvale, a small rural district. One of the teachers in the elementary school, Ms. Yoon, recently implemented a token economy in her classroom in an effort to increase prosocial behaviors among a small group of her students during cooperative learning activities. Although Ms. Yoon *thinks* that the intervention has been successful (she told Mr. Cohen that "the classroom environment feels more positive"), she would like to know for sure and asks Mr. Cohen to help her collect data to support this belief. Mr. Cohen is pleased that Ms. Yoon has sought him out and certainly wants to help, but his schedule is barely manageable over the next few weeks given other commitments. Thus, Ms. Yoon and Mr. Cohen agree to have Ms. Yoon collect data using a DBR, with Mr. Cohen coming in periodically (i.e., once per week) to supplement the DBR data with systematic direct observations.

To improve time efficiency, two additional factors should be considered when choosing to use a DBR: (1) skill level of the rater and (2) rater acceptance of the tool. Although the DBR is a very simple tool, the observer must be willing to complete the rating when asked and to do so consistently. That is, given that the classroom teacher often serves as the rater, he or she must view the DBR and the obtained data as acceptable. Enlisting an unwilling observer is a recipe for disaster! If Ms. Yoon was hesitant to use the DBR because she felt that she would have trouble remembering to complete it, it would be important to work with her to find an acceptable solution (e.g., provide a prompt for rating). If Mr. Cohen simply insists that Ms. Yoon use the DBR despite her hesitation, she may not complete it accurately or at all. In such a situation, one of the attractions of the DBR (i.e., an in-class observer) can become a significant liability. In addition, if the user also is responsible for summarizing the data, he or she must have skill in both graphing and interpreting results. In summary, understanding the level of assistance (e.g., brief demonstration of using the DBR versus extensive modeling and feedback) is an important consideration to ensure that the rater will use it effectively.

In conclusion, although further research is needed to define the critical parameters under which the DBR can be used in assessment, available evidence and the relatively low resources needed support the use of the DBR in lower-stakes decisions, particularly when repeated and frequent assessment data are needed and the raters are motivated to use the DBR.

HOW SHOULD YOU DESIGN THE DBR FORM?

Once a DBR is determined to be an appropriate tool for a given situation, the next decisions relate to designing the actual rating form. As noted, one of the most attractive aspects of the DBR is the wide variety of options for using it. Although this flexibility is certainly an advantage, the disadvantage is the lack of a single exemplar or template from which to create an individual DBR. As a result, educators must make design decisions based on the characteristics of each situation. Although this step may take some time, individualizing the rating will generate data that are appropriate and specific to the questions being asked. To facilitate making decisions about designing the DBR, we provide a series of questions to answer that are similar across all types and intended purposes of DBRs. See Table 5.1 for a quick guide to these questions.

What Is the Target Behavior and Who Is the Focus of the Rating?

As long as the behavior of interest is defined clearly and understood by the rater and consumers of the information, several options for selecting a target behavior are available (see Chapter 4 for multiple examples of target behaviors and associated definitions). For example, although we recommend a focus on appropriate or positive behaviors, the DBR can be designed to address increases in positive or appropriate behaviors or decreases in negative or inappropriate behaviors. In addition, DBRs can be designed to focus on the behaviors of an individual student, a small group of students, or the entire class. For example, whereas one teacher may want data on the inattentive behavior of a single student, another may be interested in one or more behaviors of some or all students in the class. Ms. Yoon was interested in the prosocial behavior of a small group of her students, while Mr. Rodcliff kept track of how long it took for the whole class to be ready for the first lesson of the day. As discussed in Chapter 1, answering why you need the data involves consideration of the target level (i.e., individual, class, school) of assessment.

What Scale for Rating Should Be Used?

One consideration when selecting the scale for rating is the developmental maturity of the individual being rated, particularly if the information is intended to be shared with that individual. For example, when rating students in primary grades, smiley faces can be helpful in explaining the meaning of the ratings. On the other hand, a Likert-type scale (e.g., 1–10) may be more meaningful and appropriate for older students. One potential disadvantage to a Likert-type scale is that the selected increments can restrict the range of behavior to be reported. For example, using a scale of 1–5 to indicate proportion of time actively engaged means that a rating of 5 could indicate anywhere from 80–100% of the time. So, when using a Likert-type scale, we recommend using either 10 increments or a continuous line. If a scale is inappropriate for a given situation, a checklist might be a better option (e.g., yes/no). A visual picture of the four different options can be found in Figure 5.1.

When, Where, and How Often Will Data Be Collected?

DBRs can be designed to provide feedback about behavior over a specific period of time (e.g., math class, morning) or an entire day. The time and location of the rating period should be based on when and where the problem behavior is typically reported. If Lisa is most likely to be observed staring out the window during math lessons, completing DBR ratings at multiple points throughout the entire academic day would be inefficient in tell-

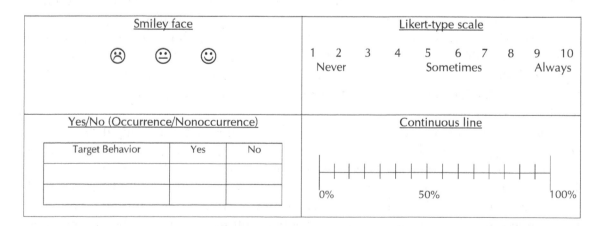

FIGURE 5.1. Options for DBR scales.

ing us about change in "staring out the window." If, on the other hand, staring is a problem for Lisa throughout the day and in several different contexts, either multiple ratings throughout the day or one overall rating for the day may be appropriate. This example also illustrates another decision that needs to be made, that is, how frequently to conduct DBR ratings. Although at least daily ratings are recommended, the information can be summarized and shared on a less frequent basis (e.g., weekly). For example, if a particular student is consistently distracting classmates through disrespectful comments during instruction, Mr. Smith may want to complete a DBR indicating how respectful the student was on a daily basis and then send this information home to the parents at the end of the week. On the other hand, if Ms. Jones wishes to monitor work completion during three daily independent work periods, she could conduct a separate rating following each period. When using the DBR to assess the effects of an intervention, the rating period should occur concurrently with the related intervention.

One final note with regard to when, where, and how often data should be collected relates to the length of time that elapses between the rating period and the actual rating. In general, the longer one waits between the end of the rating period and actual completion of the DBR, the more error the rating is likely to contain. For example, as her students leave the classroom for recess, Ms. Yoon remembers that she forgot to complete a DBR for Erin during a cooperative learning activity. Although Erin interacted well with her peers during the activity, she was particularly uncooperative during the reading lesson that followed. So, when Ms. Yoon finally sits down to complete the DBR, she gives Erin a low rating given her most recent behavior (uncooperative during reading), therefore inaccurately reporting the behavior of interest (positive peer interaction during cooperative learning). Although such daily reports are typically completed during a teacher's break or at the end of the day, a significant lapse in time between the observation period and the rating can introduce other confounding events or experiences, which can bias the rating.

Who Will Conduct the Rating?

Yet another consideration when designing the DBR is who will be responsible for conducting the rating. Most often, the person will be the classroom teacher or someone who is with the student consistently throughout the day, especially during the specified rating period. As previously noted, the burden on resources is significantly reduced when the rater is someone already present in the student's environment; however, that person must be willing and able to complete the rating as specified. Recent research findings have suggested that having the same rater be responsible for all ratings (see Chafouleas, Christ, et al., 2007; Chafouleas, Riley-Tillman, et al., 2007) is important to avoid inconsistencies across raters.

Another option is to have the student complete the rating, especially if the data are collected as part of a self-monitoring intervention. Self-monitoring involves observing and recording one's behavior (Maag, Rutherford, & DiGangi, 1992; Shapiro & Cole, 1994) and can be used in addition to or in place of a teacher rating. In addition to providing behavioral data, self-monitoring has been shown to be a powerful intervention for teaching appropriate behavior. As an intervention, self-monitoring has been used effectively for students with learning disabilities (e.g., Dalton, Martella, & Marchand-Martella, 1999; Maag et al., 1992; Todd, Horner, & Sugai, 1999), ADHD (e.g., Ardoin & Martens, 2004), and emotional and behavioral disorders (e.g., Dunlap et al., 1995), as well as for students without exceptionalities (e.g., Rock, 2005; Wood, Murdock, Cronin, Dawson, & Kirby, 1998). The appropriateness of using a DBR in self-monitoring is dependent on the child's understanding of the task and follow-through with the rating procedures. If a self-monitoring component is selected, the student must be taught to accurately self-monitor (Ardoin & Martens, 2004; Shapiro & Cole, 1994). First, students need to learn to identify when they have engaged in a behavior and understand the method that will be used to record their behavior. For example, a teacher might say the following:

> "I would like to work with you to monitor [or check] your behavior in class. We are going to rate how well you pay attention and work on assignments using a scale from 0 to 5, with 1 meaning you didn't pay attention very well and 5 meaning you paid great attention. A 2, 3, or 4 rating means that you paid attention for a little, some, or most but not all of the time. I would like you to use this card to rate your behavior after math class, and I also will rate your behavior on a separate card. After the class period, we will meet to talk about our ratings. Do you understand what we are going to do? Let's practice a couple of examples . . ."

In the initial stages, the student's rating should be compared to an adult rating (e.g., the teacher's) and should receive meaningful positive reinforcement for accuracy. Once the student's ratings are consistently similar to the teacher's ratings and the teacher is confident in the student's ability to continue rating independently, the comparison might be faded to a point where random and intermittent accuracy checks are conducted. Further suggestions for user-friendly resources on self-monitoring can be found in Table 5.2.

TABLE 5.2. User-Friendly Resources on Using DBR in Self-Management

Resource	Description
Crone, D. A., Horner, R. H., & Hawken, L. S. (2004). *Responding to problem behavior in schools: The behavior education program*. New York: Guilford Press.	In this book, a program targeting students at risk for behavior problems is described. The program involves daily rating and checking of student behavior. One option is to use self-management when fading supports.
Jenson, W. R., Rhode, G., & Reavis, H. K. (1994). *The tough kid tool box*. Longmont, CO: Sopris West.	One section of this popular intervention book for practitioners is dedicated to self-monitoring, including suggestions for troubleshooting problems.
Shapiro, E. S., & Cole, C. L. (1994). *Behavior change in the classroom: Self-management interventions*. New York: Guilford Press.	In this book, conceptual foundations of, and practical approaches for, school-based self-management interventions are offered, including interventions for students with more severe disabilities.
www.interventioncentral.org	This website offers an extensive resource on using behavior ratings in the *Classroom Behavior Report Card Manual*.

Will DBRs Be Tied to Consequences?

The two final decisions are to determine (1) whether use of a DBR will involve consequences for rated behaviors (i.e., as part of the intervention) and (2) who will be responsible for providing consequences (e.g., parent/guardian, support staff, another teacher). Individual situations dictate whether or not rewards and/or punishers should be used in conjunction with a DBR. Consequences such as positive reinforcement (e.g., praise, tangible rewards) can be added for meeting a certain goal (e.g., four smiley faces per week). The setting for delivery of contingencies may not necessarily be the classroom. For example, Mr. Charles meets with Lisa's parents to share baseline data regarding her inattentive behavior in class. They agree to an intervention plan that includes both positive verbal reinforcement as well as a home-based reinforcer involving 20 minutes of time on the telephone for each day in which she receives a high DBR rating indicating good attention. When the setting for delivery of consequences involves persons other than the rater, everyone must understand, agree upon, and follow through with delivery of the consequences (e.g., average rating of 3 = extra computer time). In some cases, a general letter about the DBR has been sent home, and rather than specifying what consequences should be used, the decision is left for the parent or guardian to make (e.g., Dougherty & Dougherty, 1977). In other cases, specific criteria for receiving consequences and clear specification of those consequences may be helpful. The decision as to whether a person other than the rater will be responsible for the delivery of consequences should be made based on the consistency with which that person is expected to follow through with the plan. If there is a possibility that consequences will not be provided regularly, another individual should be identified to assume this responsibility.

In Case Example 5.1, Ms. Greenville and Dr. Storrs develop an actual DBR. In addition, reproducible DBR forms and other resources for facilitating the development of a DBR form can be found in Appendices 5.1–5.8. Another excellent tool is the Behavior Reporter Behavior Report Card Generator, found on the Intervention Central website (*www.interventioncentral.org*), which allows a user to include demographic information, a name for the card, and customized directions. You can then select from a number of target behaviors and even input the child's name into behavior-related statements (e.g., "John wrote down homework assignments correctly and completely"). Finally, the option of creating a daily or weekly rating sheet is provided. With the click of a button, the card is created and can be printed for use. See Figure 5.2 for examples of cards created on the Intervention Central website.

WHAT SHOULD BE CONSIDERED WHEN IMPLEMENTING DBR PROCEDURES?

Once the DBR form has been constructed, implementation can begin. When the DBR is first presented to the rater, time must be allocated to discuss the procedure for completing it. This discussion should include review of the target behavior(s), how long a rating period will be, and when a rating will be completed. Once implementation has begun, several additional issues must be addressed.

CASE EXAMPLE 5.1

Ms. Greenville, a fifth-grade teacher, has reported recent difficulty with Jane, typically described as one of her "favorite" students. According to Ms. Greenville, although Jane has previously been a well-behaved and conscientious student, her behavior has changed. As a result, Ms. Greenville approached Dr. Storrs, the school psychologist, to discuss the problem and develop an intervention plan. Through discussion, it became clear that Jane's problematic behavior could be primarily defined as falling within inappropriate "calling out." In addition, Ms. Greenville explained that this behavior was most evident during writing activities. She emphasized that Jane was not having academic difficulty, and that recent assessments supported the fact that she was performing at a level expected in her class. In order to further clarify the situation, Dr. Storrs suggested that he come in to observe the class during the identified problematic times and asked that Ms. Greenville also collect some data using a DBR. Furthermore, considering that in this case a "low-stakes" decision was probably being made (developing a classroom-based intervention), the use of the DBR was determined to be appropriate.

Dr. Storrs and Ms. Greenville designed a DBR using the guiding questions presented in Table 5.1. First, although the target behavior discussed involved calling out, it was decided that the DBR would be framed in terms of desired behavior (hand raising), as well as the global behavior of time on task. Therefore, in this case, the DBR was designed to include two outcome variables. The appropriate alternative to calling out, Jane raising her hand, was defined as "the student raises her hand and is called on before responding." The general academic behavior of "on task" was defined as "the student is actively working on the assigned activity" (e.g., writing, reading aloud, discussing responses). These definitions both described the alternative behaviors from the perspective of Ms. Greenville and provided Dr. Storrs with operational definitions that could be used when conducting his observations. Considering that the referral concern pinpointed writing activities as the time and place in which the behavior problem was most evident, this period was selected as the rating period. Finally, Ms. Greenville indicated that she had experience with, and was comfortable using, a DBR involving a 10-point Likert-type scale. Armed with all of this information, Dr. Storrs created the following DBR for this case.

Student's Name: _Jane_   Date of Observation: _____

Activity: _Writing Instruction_   Time of Observation: _____

Rate the student on the degree to which she exhibited the following behaviors during writing instruction (9:00–9:30).

First Target Behavior: _Raising Hand: "The student raised her hand and was called on before responding."_

1	2	3	4	5	6	7	8	9	10
(0 Times)				(5 Times)					(10+ Times)

Second Target Behavior: _On Task: "The student was actively working on the assigned activity."_

1	2	3	4	5	6	7	8	9	10
(0–10%)	(11–20%)	(21–30%)	(31–40%)	(41–50%)	(51–60%)	(61–70%)	(71–80%)	(81–90%)	(91–100%)

(continued)

After 4 days of collecting baseline data with the DBR, Ms. Greenville and Dr. Storrs met to develop an intervention and determine implementation of the intervention and data collection schedules. Over the course of the next several weeks, Ms. Greenville collected DBR data and conducted the intervention. In addition, Dr. Storrs collected SDO data on two separate occasions during baseline, and then twice in the intervention phase. At the end of 2 weeks of intervention implementation, Ms. Greenville and Dr. Storrs met to review the data. Ms. Greenville indicated that she believed the intervention was effective. Both the DBR and SDO data supported this perception. Once Dr. Storrs graphed their findings, it became evident to both Ms. Greenville and Dr. Storrs that the intervention had been effective. Over the course of the intervention, Jane raised her hand with increasing frequency and improved her overall level of on-task behavior. Both Ms. Greenville and Dr. Storrs' data are provided below:

SDO Information (Dr. Storrs)	Percentage of intervals observed to be on task	Frequency of observed hand raising
Baseline observation Wednesday	30%	2
Intervention observation 2nd Wednesday	90%	8

DBR Ratings (Ms. Greenville)	On task	Raising hand
Baseline		
Tuesday	1	0
Wednesday	2	2
Thursday	2	1
Friday	1	2
Intervention Week 1		
Monday	5	3
Tuesday	6	3
Wednesday	8	6
Thursday	7	5
Friday	7	8
Intervention Week 2		
Monday	7	7
Tuesday	8	9
Wednesday	9	8
Thursday	9	7
Friday	10	9

(continued)

Graphs of DBR information from Ms. Greenville:

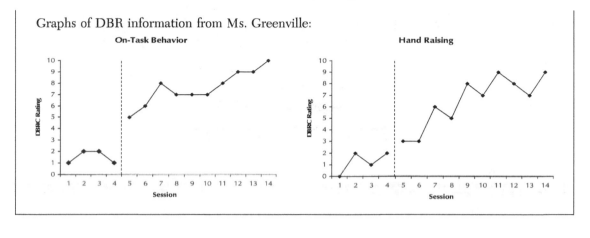

FIGURE 5.2. Examples from the Behavior Report Card Generator. Copyright 2004 by Jim Wright. Reprinted by permission from *www.interventioncentral.org*.

(continued)

The Behavior **Reporter**   On-Line Behavior Report Card Generator
A service of www.interventioncentral.org

Monitoring Charts 1 to 2 of 3

[View Next Charts >>]

Behavior Report Card

Student Name: _____

Start Date: Wk 1: __ / __ / __   Wk 2: __ / __ / __   Wk 3: __ / __ / __   Wk 4: __ / __ / __
M T W Th F   M T W Th F   M T W Th F   M T W Th F

The student focused his or her attention on teacher instructions, classroom lessons and assigned work.

	9 ○ ○ ○ ○ ○	○ ○ ○ ○ ○	9 ○ ○ ○ ○ ○	○ ○ ○ ○ ○ 9	
Usually/Always	8 ○ ○ ○ ○ ○	○ ○ ○ ○ ○	8 ○ ○ ○ ○ ○	○ ○ ○ ○ ○ 8	Usually/Always
	7 ○ ○ ○ ○ ○	○ ○ ○ ○ ○	7 ○ ○ ○ ○ ○	○ ○ ○ ○ ○ 7	
	6 ○ ○ ○ ○ ○	○ ○ ○ ○ ○	6 ○ ○ ○ ○ ○	○ ○ ○ ○ ○ 6	
Sometimes	5 ○ ○ ○ ○ ○	○ ○ ○ ○ ○	5 ○ ○ ○ ○ ○	○ ○ ○ ○ ○ 5	Sometimes
	4 ○ ○ ○ ○ ○	○ ○ ○ ○ ○	4 ○ ○ ○ ○ ○	○ ○ ○ ○ ○ 4	
	3 ○ ○ ○ ○ ○	○ ○ ○ ○ ○	3 ○ ○ ○ ○ ○	○ ○ ○ ○ ○ 3	
Never/Seldom	2 ○ ○ ○ ○ ○	○ ○ ○ ○ ○	2 ○ ○ ○ ○ ○	○ ○ ○ ○ ○ 2	Never/Seldom
	1 ○ ○ ○ ○ ○	○ ○ ○ ○ ○	1 ○ ○ ○ ○ ○	○ ○ ○ ○ ○ 1	
	M T W Th F	M T W Th F	M T W Th F	M T W Th F	

The student sat in class without fidgeting or squirming more than most peers.

	9 ○ ○ ○ ○ ○	○ ○ ○ ○ ○	9 ○ ○ ○ ○ ○	○ ○ ○ ○ ○ 9	
Usually/Always	8 ○ ○ ○ ○ ○	○ ○ ○ ○ ○	8 ○ ○ ○ ○ ○	○ ○ ○ ○ ○ 8	Usually/Always
	7 ○ ○ ○ ○ ○	○ ○ ○ ○ ○	7 ○ ○ ○ ○ ○	○ ○ ○ ○ ○ 7	
	6 ○ ○ ○ ○ ○	○ ○ ○ ○ ○	6 ○ ○ ○ ○ ○	○ ○ ○ ○ ○ 6	
Sometimes	5 ○ ○ ○ ○ ○	○ ○ ○ ○ ○	5 ○ ○ ○ ○ ○	○ ○ ○ ○ ○ 5	Sometimes
	4 ○ ○ ○ ○ ○	○ ○ ○ ○ ○	4 ○ ○ ○ ○ ○	○ ○ ○ ○ ○ 4	
	3 ○ ○ ○ ○ ○	○ ○ ○ ○ ○	3 ○ ○ ○ ○ ○	○ ○ ○ ○ ○ 3	
Never/Seldom	2 ○ ○ ○ ○ ○	○ ○ ○ ○ ○	2 ○ ○ ○ ○ ○	○ ○ ○ ○ ○ 2	Never/Seldom
	1 ○ ○ ○ ○ ○	○ ○ ○ ○ ○	1 ○ ○ ○ ○ ○	○ ○ ○ ○ ○ 1	
	M T W Th F	M T W Th F	M T W Th F	M T W Th F	

©2004 Jim Wright

FIGURE 5.2. *(continued)*

First, examining fidelity of implementation is important, that is, does the rater complete the DBR as specified? To some extent, documentation of completion will be provided by permanent products (in this case, the existence of the specified DBR or lack thereof). Although simply producing the completed DBR provides initial evidence of fidelity, other points must be considered as well. For example, was the DBR completed at the requested time of day? If the teacher was to complete the DBR immediately following an intervention scheduled from 9:00 to 9:30 daily, how will you know that it was done? Therefore, it may be important to periodically check in with the rater. If and when concerns arise, providing the rater with a prompt, such as an integrity checklist (e.g., when to complete the DBR, what time period to consider for doing the ratings), can be useful. If the rater is not completing the DBR as originally agreed, a discussion may be warranted to provide feedback and retrain and/or modify the plan.

A related consideration is whether the rater continues to find the DBR acceptable to use. One of the potential advantages of DBRs is the ease of use in comparison to other data collection methods. However, an individual teacher may not find the procedure acceptable, particularly when asked to use it consistently over time. Thus, after initial implementation, periodical assessments of acceptability can be helpful to determine if the user remains supportive of the DBR as a data collection tool.

Yet another issue relates to whether DBR data correspond with other sources of data. In the case example, data from different sources and methods corresponded, but what if they did not? In fact, most school psychologists have encountered a challenging situation in which a teacher's perception of a student's behavior and the student's behavior as measured by our assessment tools do not correspond. Numerous hypotheses are possible: (1) the student (or even the teacher) behaves differently when the school psychologist is present, (2) the teacher is measuring something other than the target behavior (e.g., he or she reduces a child's "on-task" rating when the child calls out), or (3) the teacher does not perceive a small yet positive effect that the intervention has had. All of these possibilities are feasible, and the situation provides an opportunity for clarification in a collaborative, consultative conversation.

HOW ARE DBR DATA SUMMARIZED?

The process for summarizing data collected from DBRs is consistent with that described in Chapter 4 for SDO techniques. That is, DBR data can be quantified, compared, combined, and summarized for summative and formative purposes. For example, DBR data of Susie's disruptive behavior over the week can be summarized into a statement of average daily or weekly rating (6 out of 10 points), or most likely period of high or low disruption (just before lunch) if multiple ratings per day are taken. In contrast to SDO, options for summarizing data are more limited given that DBR data are not likely to vary as much. Since DBRs involve rating on some scale, data are summarized relevant to the scale. For example, a simple yes/no checklist can be easily depicted through a bar chart whereas rating information might be plotted on a line graph, with the intervals on the y axis indicating the DBR scale. See Case Example 5.1 for an example of a line graph as well as Appendix 5.8 for a blank graph with a 10-point scale.

WHAT ARE THE STRENGTHS OF DBRs?

Highly Flexible

As previously mentioned, perhaps one of the most attractive features of a DBR is the broad array of uses and applications. For example, DBRs can be used with preschool through high school populations to provide information about positive and negative behaviors. In addition, they can be used to monitor a wide range of behaviors, from assignment completion to physical aggression. Finally, they can be used to rate one individual or a larger group. This flexibility is an important strength of DBRs in that one common tool can be used to fit the needs of a variety of educational situations.

Additionally, DBRs can be used with behaviors that are difficult for an external observer to observe directly. Most notably, low-frequency behaviors (e.g., enuresis, violent outbursts) are unlikely to be observed in a random 10 minute observation. In such cases, "observers" who are always present in the classroom environment can be used to rate behaviors. An additional potential benefit of a DBR is the ability to measure clusters of behavior in much the same way that behavior rating scales do. For example, if Mrs. Sanchez wishes to monitor Alexa's "aggressive" behavior, she can construct a DBR in which the target behavior is a cluster that represents aggression (e.g., Alexa kept her hands to herself, Alexa did not make any threats toward her peers, Alexa avoided physical encounters with her peers). However, although DBRs can be used to measure clusters of behaviors, it is important to note that the technical characteristics (i.e. reliability and validity) of doing so are not yet fully understood.

Highly Feasible, Acceptable, and Familiar

Generally, educators are familiar with and have been found to use a tool such as the DBR. Survey results have suggested teachers are accepting of the DBR as a tool in both intervention and assessment (Chafouleas et al., 2006). Results of another study suggested school psychologists' acceptance of using a DBR as an intervention monitoring tool was similar to that for SDO (Riley-Tillman, Chafouleas, & Eckert, 2006). These findings related to feasibility, acceptability, and familiarity are encouraging in that asking teachers to use DBRs may be an efficient way to collect assessment data without significant disruption to the existing environment. For example, given familiarity with the tool, preparation (i.e., training and adaptations) for incorporating DBRs into daily practice may be minimal.

High Potential for Use in Progress Monitoring

DBRs can be created to include the characteristics identified as desirable for measures used in progress monitoring (see Jenkins, Deno, & Mirkin, 1979). DBRs are (1) constructed in a manner so as to be tied to behavioral expectations, (2) administered quickly, (3) available in multiple forms, (4) inexpensive, and (5) constructed to be completed immediately following a rating period. Together, these characteristics place the DBR on the direct end of the continuum of behavior assessment tools. With increased demands for outcome-oriented behavioral assessment and intervention planning, DBRs represent potentially viable tools for developing student goals, monitoring student progress, administering and evaluating intervention components, and increasing communication between school and home.

Reduced Risk of Reactivity

One concern related to DBRs is the potential effect of an external observer on teacher and student behavior, that is, the increased probability that the teacher and students will behave in atypical ways. This phenomenon is referred to as a *reactivity effect*. The use of a DBR has the potential to produce a reactivity effect, but in a different way. Research has suggested that asking teachers to conduct ratings may increase the rate of prompts and/or positive feedback to the target student (i.e., completing the DBR itself is a prompt for the teacher to attend to student behavior; Hey, Nelson & Hay, 1977, 1980). The main difference between the impact of using a DBR and the impact of an external observer is that the DBR can be used continuously throughout the day whereas the observer will enter and leave the setting over the designated time periods. In the end, although reactivity must be considered with both observation strategies, the effect may be more favorable over the long term when using the DBR.

Can Be Used in Both Assessment and Intervention

An important benefit of using a DBR is simultaneous use in intervention. When the DBR is used as an intervention (e.g., self-monitoring), DBR information can be used as assessment data related to progress monitoring. Self-monitoring has been found to be an effective intervention for a number of outcome variables, including work completion (Piersel, 1985) and disruptive behavior (Smith, Young, West, Morgan, & Rhode, 1988). Researchers have suggested that the simple act of raising an individual's awareness of his or her own behavior may serve to significantly alter behavior. This potential dual role further highlights the feasibility of DBRs for use in applied settings.

Minimal Cost for Materials

Like direct observation, DBRs are appealing because they are relatively inexpensive. For teacher-developed ratings, DBR costs are associated with paper, writing utensils, and use of a common software program. The main cost is the time needed to define what behaviors are to be rated and how the DBR procedures will be implemented.

WHAT ARE THE WEAKNESSES OF DBRs?

Rater Influence

As previously discussed, the influence of raters on DBR data is not yet fully understood. Like all forms of behavioral assessment, a DBR may be a less accurate estimate of the student's actual behavior during the specified rating period. That is, given that the DBR rater is often someone who is familiar with the student, history may influence rating to a greater degree than data collection involving an external person who is not familiar with the student.

Sattler (2002) reported that DBR forms of rating suffer from low reliability, scale issues, and central tendency/halo effects. Additionally, a time delay between the observation and the recording could reduce the accuracy of the rating. For example, in many situations, the teacher may be unable to complete a DBR rating until a lull in activity or a later transition period.

Limited Response Format

The response format of a DBR (e.g., a Likert-type scale from 1 to 10) inevitably lessens sensitivity to change more than SDO. Whereas most formats for SDO allow for rating of behavior on a continuous scale from 0% to 100%, most DBRs limit the number of response options by clustering. For example, with a response option in which a rating of 1 represents behavior occurring from 0% to 19% of the time, the range restriction serves to give the same score to a student who does not exhibit the target behavior at all and a student who exhibits the target behavior approximately one fifth of the time.

Limited Knowledge about Psychometric Adequacy

As previously noted, systematic attention has recently been directed toward examining the psychometric adequacy of the DBR for various assessment purposes, and supporting evidence is emerging. Although the advantages of DBRs are encouraging, especially in applied settings, users should be conservative in their use of DBRs across all assessment purposes. Collecting additional forms of data is recommended to corroborate DBR-based decisions.

CONCLUDING COMMENTS

In this chapter, we provided an overview of the DBR as a behavioral assessment tool, with emphasis on its potential for use in behavior monitoring. In summary, the DBR may be a useful addition to an assessment battery given its feasibility and flexibility. However, although flexibility is strength, adherence to standardized procedures for use is important. As further empirical attention is directed toward the DBR as an assessment tool, more concrete recommendations for use will become available. Obviously, use of a DBR is not appropriate in every situation, and this chapter has provided a process for guiding decisions about appropriateness, along with examples regarding creating, implementing, and summarizing DBR data.

BLANK DBR USING A SMILEY-FACE SCALE

Child Name: _____

Date: _____

Today, this is how well the student

_____

(List specific behavior here.)

During _____

During _____

During _____

BLANK WEEKLY DBR USING A SMILEY-FACE SCALE

	Monday	Tuesday	Wednesday	Thursday	Friday
Student _____ (Specify behavior here.) 😊 😐 😞					
Student _____ (Specify behavior here.) 😊 😐 😞					
Student _____ (Specify behavior here.) 😊 😐 😞					
Student _____ (Specify behavior here.) 😊 😐 😞					

Comments: _____

_____

_____

BLANK DBR USING A LIKERT-TYPE SCALE

Student's Name: _____   Date: _____

Setting: _____   Time: _____

Compared with other students in the classroom, the student:

1	2	3	4	5	6	7	8	9	10
Never					Occasionally				Always

1	2	3	4	5	6	7	8	9	10
Never					Occasionally				Always

1	2	3	4	5	6	7	8	9	10
Never					Occasionally				Always

Comments:

BLANK WEEKLY DBR USING A LIKERT-TYPE SCALE

	Monday	Tuesday	Wednesday	Thursday	Friday
Student _____ _____ (Specify behavior here.) 1 2 3 4 5 6 7 8 9 10 Never Occasionally Always					
Student _____ _____ (Specify behavior here.) 1 2 3 4 5 6 7 8 9 10 Never Occasionally Always					
Student _____ _____ (Specify behavior here.) 1 2 3 4 5 6 7 8 9 10 Never Occasionally Always					
Student _____ _____ (Specify behavior here.) 1 2 3 4 5 6 7 8 9 10 Never Occasionally Always					

BLANK DBR USING A CONTINUOUS LINE SCALE

Date: _____

Teacher: _____

Rating Activity/Time: _____

DIRECTIONS: Place a dot along the line that best reflects the *proportion of time the target student was engaged in the target behavior over the rating period*. Specific behaviors to be rated are as follows:

_____ : _____
(Behavior)   (Operational definition)

_____ : _____
(Behavior)   (Operational definition)

Target Student's Name: _____

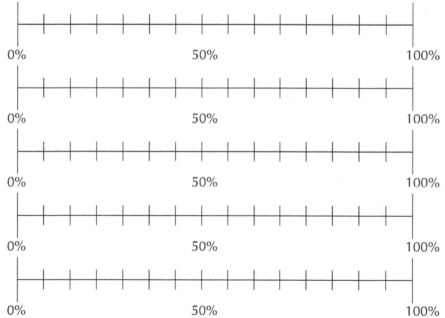

BLANK DBR USING A CHECKLIST FORMAT

Student's Name: _____

Date: _____

Target Behavior	Yes	No

Comments: _____

_____

_____

_____

_____

_____

_____

_____

_____

_____

_____

BLANK WEEKLY DBR USING A CHECKLIST FORMAT

	Monday	Tuesday	Wednesday	Thursday	Friday
_____ (student's name) _____ (Specify behavior here.)	Y / N	Y / N	Y / N	Y / N	Y / N
_____ (student's name) _____ (Specify behavior here.)	Y / N	Y / N	Y / N	Y / N	Y / N
_____ (student's name) _____ (Specify behavior here.)	Y / N	Y / N	Y / N	Y / N	Y / N
_____ (student's name) _____ (Specify behavior here.)	Y / N	Y / N	Y / N	Y / N	Y / N

RECORDING GRAPH

Student's Name: _____   Teacher: _____

Dates Administered: _____

Sessions

6

Behavior Rating Scales

One of the main reasons that assessment data are collected is to understand behavior so that generalizable or global statements can be made about a student's behavior. For example, a psychologist may want an estimate of how a particular student *typically* behaves in a setting. Rather than out-of-seat and calling-out behavior during instructional time on Tuesdays, information about typical behavior in school related to a category of "disruption" may be of interest. In this chapter, we review behavior rating scales, which are tools that are designed to reliably measure a cluster of related behaviors. In this review, we discuss some examples of specific behavior rating scales with an emphasis on making decisions regarding their use.

WHAT ARE BEHAVIOR RATING SCALES AND WHY USE THEM?

Behavior rating scales are assessment tools that require one to rate the behavior of another based on past observation (Kratochwill, Sheridan, Carlson, & Lasecki, 1999). In schools, although teachers and students may rate their own behavior, we most often identify the rater as the teacher or parent and the "another" as the student. One criterion for completing a behavior rating scale is that the rater be familiar with the student. Specific definitions of familiarity (e.g., 6 months) may or may not be provided within the directions for using a scale. Ratings are conducted following the actual observations of behavior and most often involve a rating of *typical* behavior over a period of some duration (e.g., over the past 2 weeks). Thus, a behavior rating scale should be considered an "indirect" measure of actual behavior, and information from a single rating scale should not be used as the sole data source in high-stakes decisions. Within this broad definition of behavior rating scales, several additional considerations emerge.

First, behavior rating scales can be considered either comprehensive or specific. *Comprehensive* scales generally comprise large number of items (often 100+) that cluster together to assess a wide range of behaviors. For example, these measures might include broad-band syndromes, such as externalizing and internalizing problems, as well as narrow-band subscales, such as attention, aggression, and adaptive behaviors (Ramsey,

Reynolds & Kamphaus, 2002). Merrell (2003) used the term "general purpose" to describe this type of behavior rating scale. In contrast, the *specific* type of behavior rating scale is focused on one or two behavioral constructs, such as what might be included within a narrow-band subscale. For example, the scale could be designed to assess attention (Brown ADD Scales; Brown, 2001) or adaptive behavior (Vineland-II; Sparrow, Cicchetti, & Balla, 1984).

Second, behavior rating scales are generally used to provide a picture of student behavior in comparison to a standard. The standard is determined by the normative sample of the scale, and generally a range of classification categories are indicated (e.g., *significantly below average, below average, average, above average, significantly above average*, or *clinical, borderline [at risk], typical*). In most scales, raw scores are converted to T scores ($M = 50$, $SD = 10$) to make this comparison, and comparisons may be done according to a variety of characteristics, such as age, grade, gender, or ethnicity. Essentially, when completing a behavior rating scale, the rater responds to a series of items about a student, for example, the degree to which a student "works independently" on a scale from 1 (never) to 4 (always). Related items cluster together to form a construct, and those ratings are compared to a normative sample. For example, a scale might include 10 individual items that assess "attentiveness." The ratings from those 10 items would be combined and compared to the normative sample to provide an indicator of that student's attentiveness in relation to what would typically be expected in a student of the same age and/or gender. It is important to note that information obtained from behavior rating scales is impacted by rater perception, in that the rater responds to the items based on how he or she perceives the student's behavior. In summary, information gleaned from behavior rating scales is based on a rater's *perception* of a student with regard to a *cluster* of behaviors and in *comparison* to some norm group. Each of these terms (*perception, cluster, comparison*) deserves additional consideration as each has an influence on the appropriateness of selecting behavior rating scales for use in various purposes for behavioral assessment.

Perception

Behavior rating scales require an individual to rate the student's behavior based on previous observations and interactions. The assumption is that raters will have sufficient knowledge to be able to provide a general rating about the student's behavior. More importantly, the assumption is that this knowledge is accurate and similar to how others with similar knowledge might rate the student's behavior. Merrell (2000, 2003) indicated that behavior rating scales are vulnerable to error from a number of sources. For example, *response bias* refers to measurement error produced by the rater. This bias can be associated with ratings that are (1) positive or negative based on unrelated characteristics (halo effect), (2) overly generous or overly critical (leniency or severity effect), and/or (3) consistently at the midpoints and avoiding the endpoints of a scale (central tendency effects). In addition, the temporal occurrence of unusual behavior is important to note when asking raters to complete a behavior rating scale. Worthen, Borg, and White (1993) indicate that raters tend to remember unusual rather than ordinary behavior. Thus uneventful behavior (e.g., quietly completing an assigned task) may not be as heavily considered when rating. For example, when a teacher is asked to rate John's aggressive behavior over the past month, the teacher is more likely to rate more severe behavior, especially at the end of the day when John had thrown a desk and punched a student! Error variance is related to response bias and provides a more general representation of the measurement problems associated with rating scales (Merrell, 2003). Four types of error variance are frequently noted: (1) source variance (e.g., different raters respond to different ways to the rating format), (2) setting variance (e.g., behavior may be present in one but not all environments), (3) temporal variance (e.g., behavior changes over time, rater changes approach to rating over time), and (4) instrument variance (e.g., rating difference across two different scales intended to measure similar constructs).

In summary, the term perception actually refers to a myriad of possible sources of error when using behavior rating scales. Thus, we should not assume that all ratings provide accurate pictures of student behavior, nor should we assume that ratings will be consistent across raters, settings, or time. A brief summary of research findings regarding cross-informant ratings (Merrell, 2000) can be found in Table 6.1. Behavior rating scales should not necessarily be considered unreliable assessment tools; however, we should expect obtained data to vary across raters.

Cluster

Behavior rating scales comprise a series of items that cluster together under one or more scales. Each presented item is rated on some continuum (e.g., "Never," "Rarely," "Sometimes," or "Often"). For example, each of the items indicated in Figure 6.1 could be grouped under the general term *attention*. Although asking the teacher about the typical attentive or inattentive behaviors of the target student would be simple, the inclusion of several items to describe attention has a number of potential advantages. First, when multiple items cluster around a given construct, our confidence in what we are rating and in the quality of the assessment tool increases. The items that make up the scales of current well-established behavior rating scales have been extensively examined with appropriate normative samples and thus are empirically based (see Achenbach & Edelbrock, 1978, for a seminal review of this process). Good psychometric evidence is important when selecting a behavior rating scale. A second potential benefit to using behavior rating scales is that descriptions of a child's behavior in applied settings often are associated with terms related to a cluster rather than a specific behavior. For example, a student may

---

TABLE 6.1. General Findings Regarding Behavior Rating Scales across Informants

- Generally, correlations of behavior ratings across raters are modest.
- Agreement in ratings across raters (two teachers) in similar roles is likely to be higher than agreement across those in dissimilar roles (parent and teacher).
- Agreement across ratings is higher for externalizing problems than internalizing problems.
- Correlations between self-report (child/adolescent) and adult raters are typically low.
- Gender of rater or student does not appear to be an important factor across raters.
- Age of student may be important, but the specific influence is not yet understood.

Note. Based on Merrell (2000).

Instructions: Circle the number next to each item that best describes this student's behavior over the past six months.

Item	Never	Rarely	Sometimes	Often
1. Is easily distracted	0	1	2	3
2. Does not finish assignments	0	1	2	3
3. Listens carefully	0	1	2	3
4. Daydreams	0	1	2	3

FIGURE 6.1. Hypothetical example of a rating scale for attention.

be described as "hyperactive" rather than "exhibits high rates of fidgeting behavior." Thus, a rating scale provides a common understanding of the specific behaviors that are indicative of a given cluster term. In turn, the term's effectiveness in communication about specific targets of intervention increases. For example, when a student is referred by the teacher for excessive displays of hyperactivity, information about ratings on specific items under the cluster "hyperactivity" can help specify the target of intervention. Different intervention plans would be warranted based on the extent to which hyperactivity is represented by "trouble staying in seat," "disrupting other children when working," or "cannot wait to take turn."

Comparison

An individual student's responses to a behavior rating scale are compared to the responses of students who make up the norm group. Ideally, this normative group includes a representative sample of the population to which we hope to generalize our findings. For most comprehensive behavior rating scales, this group is representative of students from across the United States, and tends to be rather large (e.g., thousands) and stratified to ensure that a number of key factors (e.g., socioeconomic status, geography, gender) are sufficiently represented. Comparison across individuals can be useful in understanding how a student's behavior compares to what typically might be expected. For example, comparing a student's hyperactivity ratings to the ratings of others his age provides a quick indication of the extent to which hyperactivity is a concern. Such information can be useful in assessment purposes involving screening and evaluation. However, comparisons across individuals (interindividual or nomothetic) rather than within an individual (intraindividual or ideographic) may not be as useful when the goal is to assess incremental behavior change over shorter periods of time.

WHEN SHOULD A BEHAVIOR RATING SCALE BE USED?

To use a behavior rating scale, you need to know the reason you require data. For example, if you are evaluating the effects of a yearlong program for teaching social skills to a group of at-risk students, pretest–posttest administration of behavior rating scales might provide relevant information to complete the evaluation. However, if the data are needed in order to modify the social skills program as each lesson is conducted, behavior rating scales may not be the best choice. The decision to use a behavior rating scale should relate to whether the obtained information can be practically meaningful for the intended purpose.

Behavior rating scales may be particularly suited for use in screening and evaluation. However, when data on a large number of students are needed, costs such as those associated with time, materials, and personnel must be considered. For example, when assessing the effects of implementing positive behavior supports across the whole school, collecting information on each student using a comprehensive behavior rating scale wouldn't be practical. In contrast, when screening to identify students at risk for behavioral difficulties, it may be more efficient to begin with an existing data source (e.g., office discipline referrals) or teacher nomination and then administer behavior rating scales to that smaller number of students to identify degree of risk.

Although behavior rating scales may be most commonly associated with diagnostic assessment, the assessment data should be linked to efficient and effective intervention. Data gleaned from behavior rating scales can be helpful in communicating about terms that describe behavior, which also facilitates decisions about where to focus intervention efforts. For example, when a teacher describes Susie as "highly aggressive," completion of a behavior rating scale can further define problem areas and narrow the specificity of intervention efforts. In Susie's case, additional information reveals that her verbal threats to peers when she doesn't get her way are more problematic than physical forms of aggression. In addition, behavior rating scale data may pinpoint appropriate target settings by indicating under what conditions behavior is more and less likely to be observed. At the level of tertiary assessment and intervention, behavior rating scale data can be helpful in generating hypotheses about the behavior that can guide further assessment and/or intervention (see Case Example 6.1).

It is important to note that elevated scores on a scale do not necessarily mean clinical diagnosis (e.g., ADHD, major depression) is warranted. Such scores indicate a look at the specific items that suggest a particular diagnosis and the collection of other validating forms of data. Additionally, because the terms used to describe a scale (e.g., hyperactivity, aggression) are selected by authors of a particular scale as a way to define the items falling under that cluster, specific items should be carefully examined rather than assuming that the same term has similar meaning across different rating scales.

With regard to progress monitoring, conclusive statements cannot be made because the development and use of behavior rating scales are relatively new over the past few decades. Merrell (2000) noted that the use of behavior rating scales in intervention planning and progress monitoring has received little empirical attention, and recommendations tend to be based on practical suggestions rather than specific empirical evidence. Use in progress monitoring is limited for a number of other reasons. First, progress monitoring typically involves intraindividual rather than interindividual comparison. When using behavior rating scales, normative comparisons are made about student behavior (interindividual) rather than about pre- and postintervention (intraindividual). Second, information from most behavior rating scales represents a generalized estimate of behavior over a period of time. Such data may not be sensitive to small changes in behavior, which may restrict use in day-to-day instructional decisions. For example, if Susie was

CASE EXAMPLE 6.1

Mr. James, a fifth-grade teacher, recently made a referral to his school's prereferral intervention team. He expressed concern about one of the students in his class, Karen, whom he describes as "always off in space." When asked to state his concern more specifically, Mr. James explained that Karen is often doodling or staring out the window when she should be doing schoolwork, and she is often out of her seat. When he has spoken with Karen about these behaviors, she has became "very defensive, sometimes even to the point of anger." The school psychologist volunteered to collect some baseline observational data about Karen's behavior in order to design an appropriate intervention plan. In addition to classroom observations, the school psychologist asked both Mr. James and Karen's mother to complete the BASC-2 Parent and Teacher Rating Forms. The obtained data (both in tabular and graphic forms) are presented below:

Summary of *T* Scores on BASC-2, Parent and Teacher Scales

	Parent	Teacher
Externalizing problems		
Hyperactivity	49	66*
Aggression	47	57
Conduct problems	52	57
Internalizing problems		
Anxiety	34	48
Depression	45	53
Somatization	35	54
School problems		
Attention problems	71	**70**
Learning problems	—	66*
Other problems		
Atypicality	58	59
Withdrawal	42	52
Adaptive skills		
Adaptability	36*	39*
Social skills	31*	**22**
Leadership	35*	42
Study skills	43	34*
Functional communication	48	47

Note. **Bold** = clinically significant (70+ on clinical, 30– on adaptive).
* = at risk (60–69 on clinical, 31–40 on adaptive).

(continued)

BASC-2 Clinical Scales

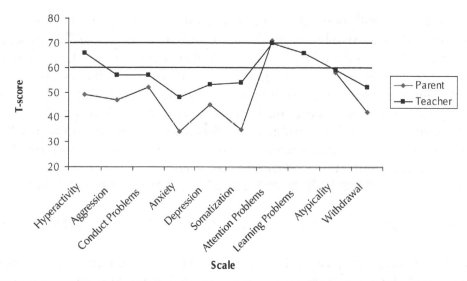

Note. Scores above the upper line (*T* score of 70 or more) are considered in the clinical range while scores above the lower line (*T* score of 60 or more) are considered in the at-risk range.

BASC-2 Adaptive Scales

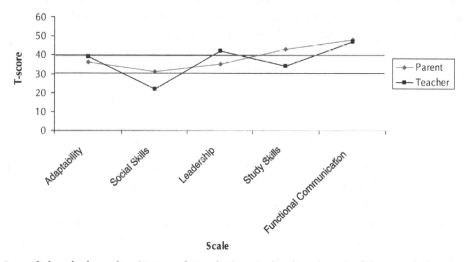

Note. Scores below the lower line (*T* score of 30 or less) are in the clinical range while scores below the upper line (*T* score of 40 or less) are considered in the at-risk range.

Results of the BASC-2 scales indicate that attention is a significant concern for Karen across settings (both in school and at home). In addition, Mr. James rated Karen in the at-risk range for issues of hyperactivity, learning problems, and study skills. In addition, the elevated learning problems and study skills scores suggest that Karen's difficulty is impacting her educational progress. Finally, the Adaptive Scales support this with scores in the clinical range in social skills (parent rater) and in the at-risk range for adaptability, social skills (parent rater), leadership (parent rater), and study skills (teacher rater). Assuming that the school psychologist finds similar patterns during observation sessions, Mr. James's concerns appear warranted in thatinterventions efforts should focus on improving Karen's attention to task, and perhaps the efforts could be expanded to include both school and home settings. It will be important for this intervention to take into consideration the reported hyperactivity issues as well as the reported adaptive and educational issues.

initially rated in the 99th percentile on items measuring aggression, even with a significant reduction in aggressive behavior, she might still be rated in the "highly aggressive" range. This situation could lead to the inappropriate conclusion that the intervention was unsuccessful, even though a meaningful reduction in aggressive behavior occurred. Third, although the time (e.g., 15–20 minutes) required to complete a behavior rating scale may be acceptable with occasional use, the time needed with repeated administrations of behavior rating scales is problematic. For example, administration of a 20-minute behavior rating scale for three students once a week for 6 weeks requires 6 hours of teacher time and is unlikely to be favorably received.

WHAT ARE SOME OF THE AVAILABLE BEHAVIOR RATING SCALES?

In general, selecting a behavior rating scale involves, for example, consideration of the behaviors sampled, normed respondent age range and characteristics, psychometric evidence of reliability and validity, feasibility and ease of use, and currency of recent versions. Although a full review of existing behavior rating scales is beyond the scope of this chapter, we describe two examples to illustrate what to look for when choosing a behavior rating scale: (1) Behavior Assessment System for Children, Second Edition (BASC-2; Reynolds & Kamphaus, 2004a) and (2) ADHD Rating Scale–IV (ADHD-IV; DuPaul, Power, Anastopoulos, & Reid, 1998). The BASC-2 exemplifies a comprehensive behavior rating scale system, whereas the ADHD-IV is an example of a specific topic behavior scale.

Behavior Assessment System for Children, Second Edition

The BASC-2 is a general-purpose behavior rating system authored by Reynolds and Kamphaus (2004) and published by AGS Publishing (*www.agsnet.com*). The BASC-2 is a well-established system with a number of different measures. In terms of comprehensive rating scales, the BASC-2 includes nine forms, with selection based on student age and rater. Three versions (preschool, child, and adolescent) of the Teacher Rating Scales (TRS) and Parent Rating Scales (PRS) are available, as well as three versions (child, adolescent and young adults attending postsecondary school) of the Self-Report of Personality (SRP). The preschool, child, and adolescent versions of the TRS and PRS are designed for use with children/young adults ages 2–5, 6–11, and 12–21, respectively. The versions of the SRP for children, adolescents, and young adults attending postsecondary school are designed for use with children/young adults ages 8–11, 12–21, and 18–25, respectively. The TRS and PRS use a 4-point Likert scale (N for never, O for often, S for sometimes, and A for almost always), whereas the SRP has a true/false question format. These questions are combined to form 16 (TRS and PRS) to 18 (SRP) subscales. TRS/PRS scales include: Activities of Daily Living, Adaptability, Aggression, Anxiety, Attention Problems, Atypicality, Conduct Problems, Depression, Functional Communication, Hyperactivity, Leadership, Learning Problems, Social Skills, Somatization, Study Skills, and Withdrawal. SRP scales include: Alcohol Abuse, Anxiety, Attention Problems, Attitude to School, Attitude to Teachers, Atypicality, Depression, Hyperactivity, Interpersonal Relations, Locus of Control, Relations with Parents, School Maladjustment, Self-Esteem, Self-Reliance, Sensation Seeking, Sense of Inadequacy, Social Stress, and Somatization.

In addition to the comprehensive forms, the BASC-2 offers a student observation system, a developmental history form, and the BASC Monitor for ADHD. The BASC Monitor is a shorter scale designed to repeatedly measure the symptoms of ADHD and gauge the impact of treatment on symptoms over time. Specifically, the BASC Monitor includes Attention Problems, Hyperactivity, Internalizing Problems and Adaptive Behavior scales. The BASC Monitor includes both teacher (TMR) and parent (PMR) versions and is suitable for students 4–18 years old.

In terms of feasibility issues, all versions of the BASC-2 comprehensive rating scales are rather extensive in terms of total number of items (100–139 items on the TRS, 134–150 items on the PRS, and 139–185 items on the SRP), and thus it is one of the longest rating scales to complete. In addition, although the BASC Monitor is described as a brief scale, the teacher and parent versions still consist of 47 and 46 items, respectively (Jones, 2001). As a result, one can expect to spend a good deal of time completing any version of the BASC. Fortunately, computer scoring is available to facilitate scoring and interpretation. In addition, both English and Spanish translations are available.

In terms of its technical characteristics, the BASC-2 had a large norm sample that was demographically controlled. In addition, the BASC-2 manual presents strong internal consistency, with interrater, test–retest, and reliability evidence. Finally, the authors of the BASC-2 present three forms of evidence about the validity of the scales (factor analytic evidence, correlations with other measures of behavior, and score profiles of clinical populations). The BASC Monitor questions were selected from the full comprehensive BASC (not the current BASC-2), and therefore normative data, as well as reliability and validity evidence, are derived from the original data. The norm sample has been described as an adequate sample of the United States population (Jones, 2001). The BASC Monitor manual provides extensive information on the reliability and validity of the instrument (Glenn, 2001). It is important to note that evidence of BASC Monitor's sensitivity to change is still needed (Angello et al., 2003). Thus, conclusions about its use in progress monitoring (the intended purpose) cannot be drawn at this time.

Given the extensive effort expended during its development and revision, the BASC-2 likely will remain one of the most used behavior rating scale instruments. Like other comprehensive rating systems, it provides a range of forms so that it can be useful with many different issues. Of course, this range comes at a cost in terms of the number of questions.

ADHD Rating Scale–IV

The ADHD-IV is an ADHD-specific short rating scale authored by DuPaul et al. (1998) and published by The Guilford Press (see *www.guilford.com*). In contrast to the vast number of options that the BASC-2 offers, this measure was built for one specific purpose, the identification of behaviors that would suggest a diagnosis of ADHD (Jenkins, 2003). Although it is more limited in scope than the BASC-2, the specific focus of the ADHD-IV provides a significant advantage in terms of feasibility. Simply put, the ADHD-IV is brief enough to be administered once easily, and reviewers have noted that the brevity of the form *may* make it a feasible tool for progress monitoring (Angello et al., 2003). However, further research is necessary before any definitive claims can be made.

The ADHD-IV includes both home and school forms that are suitable for students ages 5 to 18 years. Questions on the ADHD-IV use a 4-point scale ranging from 0 (never or rarely) to 3 (very often) and are used to build two subscales (Inattention and Hyperactivity-Impulsivity) that are directly linked to the subtypes of ADHD in the *Diagnostic and Statistical Manual of Mental Disorders, Fourth Edition, Text Revision* (American Psychiatric Association, 2000). Norm samples for both the home and school versions included 2,000 children and were designed to approximate the 1990 U.S. Census data for ethnic group and region of residence (Lindskog, 2003). Psychometric properties (e.g., stability and internal consistency) have been described as strong (Angello et. al., 2003), and exploratory and confirmatory factor analyses have supported both an overall one-factor model for ADHD as well as a hyperactive/impulsivity and inattention two-factor model (DuPaul et al., 1997, 1998). Reviewers have described validity evidence (concurrent, discriminate, and predictive) as acceptable (Jenkins, 2001). The samples used to assess validity are not comprehensive, in that they sampled only children 5–14 years old (rather than 5–18).

The BASC-2 system and the ADHD-IV represent two ends of the spectrum of available options. More information about specific systems is available in Kenneth Merrell's book *Behavioral, Social, and Emotional Assessment of Children and Adolescents, Second Edition* (2003). Information about narrow short scales like the ADHD-IV is available in Angello and colleagues' (2003) review of six published rating scales. These two publications provide a wealth of information about the more common systems and narrow scales.

HOW DO YOU SUMMARIZE DATA COLLECTED FROM BEHAVIOR RATING SCALES?

Options for summarizing data collected from behavior rating scales are restricted by the type of data obtained. As previously noted, raw scores on most behavior rating scales are converted to *t* scores based on age and/or gender comparisons. This standardized information is then used in interpretation of behavior. Typically, data are presented in tabular or graphical form comparing a student's *T* scores across each scale. Case Example 6.2 highlights the general utility of this type of tool and how the outcome data might be presented.

WHAT ARE THE STRENGTHS ASSOCIATED WITH BEHAVIOR RATING SCALES?

Reliable Estimates of Multiple Behaviors

Many behavior rating scales show evidence of good technical properties. Thus, these scales can be valuable for use in identifying the prevalence and severity of clusters of behavior. Reliable global information about an individual's behavior can be useful in determining next steps in assessment and/or intervention.

CASE EXAMPLE 6.2

In January Ms. Wilson decided to implement a classwide behavior management system in her 4th-grade class. In addition to looking for change at the classwide level, she is interested in determining the impact of the system on the behavior of one particular student, Chris. In this situation, behavior rating scales could be used as one tool for outcome data. The options for summarizing data, however, will depend on which scales are utilized and whether these scales have been administered in the past. In Chris's case, both his classroom teacher and his parents had completed a Conners' Rating Scales—Revised (CRS-R) Long Form early the previous year due to concerns about behavior described as inattentive and hyperactive. Thus Ms. Wilson could use this information to derive a general estimate of Chris's functioning at the beginning of the school year (see table below). Then, completion of the scales again at the end of the classwide intervention can provide information that can be used in evaluation.

Results of Conners' Rating Scales for Chris—Beginning of Fall Semester

Subscale/index	Teacher version		Parent version	
	T score	Level	T score	Level
Oppositional	48	Average	52	Average
Cognitive Problems/Inattention	61	Mildly Atypical	64	Mildly Atypical
Hyperactivity	67	Moderately Atypical	61	Mildly Atypical
Anxious–Shy	52	Average	49	Average
Perfectionism	44	Mildly Atypical	42	Mildly Atypical
Social Problems	58	Mildly Atypical	55	Average
Psychosomatic	—	—	50	Average
ADHD Index	59	Mildly Atypical	63	Mildly Atypical
Global Index	54	Average	53	Average

Results of Conners' Rating Scales for Chris—Spring Semester, Following Classwide Intervention

Subscale/index	Teacher version		Parent version	
	T score	Level	T score	Level
Oppositional	48	Average	45	Average
Cognitive Problems/Inattention	55	Average	56	Mildly Atypical
Hyperactivity	48	Average	53	Average
Anxious–Shy	52	Average	48	Average
Perfectionism	47	Average	45	Average
Social Problems	51	Average	55	Average
Psychosomatic	—	—	50	Average
ADHD Index	52	Average	54	Average
Global Index	52	Average	53	Average

Note. Scores are reported as *T* scores, which have a mean of 50, and a standard deviation of 10. In general, higher *T* scores are associated with more problems or a higher frequency of problems. *T* scores above 65 indicate clinically significant problems.

Although Chris's behavior was not highly problematic (i.e., clinically significant) according to the behavior rating scale results obtained in the fall, some concern regarding inattentive/hyperactive behavior was confirmed—but a decision was made not to develop an individualized intervention at that time. Following implementation of a classwide intervention designed

(continued)

to increase attention, results of the behavior rating scales suggested that Chris's behavior fell in the more typical range in comparison to peers. However, before drawing any final conclusions, it is important to note exactly what these scores do and do not suggest. The scores suggest that, according to the raters, Chris's behavior had become more typical in relation to what would be expected over the course of the year. Although one explanation for the change could be the classwide intervention, it is not possible to definitively confirm this with these data. Regardless of the specific cause(s), this source of data does tell us that we may no longer need to be concerned about his behavior. Assuming consistent findings from other data sources (e.g., teacher/parent report, permanent products such as grades), Chris's case could be set aside to focus on more problematic cases requiring intensive intervention.

Use for Screening, Diagnostic, and Evaluative Purposes

An important strength of behavior rating scales is the capacity for interindividual comparison when the concern is on current progress compared to what would be expected. Such information can be useful when deciding whether an intervention is needed, where intervention efforts might best be focused, and whether desired outcomes are being achieved. Information obtained from behavior rating scales can provide a structured overview of raters' perceptions of a student's behavior, which, in turn, may be useful in the development of behavioral interventions (Nelson, Benner, Reid, Epstein, & Currin, 2002). However, this information may be more useful for preintervention exploration of a student's behavior (Sandoval & Echandia, 1994) than for the creation of specific intervention strategies.

Feasibility When Administered Infrequently

The commitment involved in using behavior rating scales is generally minimal when they are administered infrequently. Although little training is needed for a rater to complete the scale, the person interpreting the information must have prior training and experience. Although completion of a comprehensive scale may take 20 minutes or more, this time is relatively short in comparison to other sources that obtain a similar volume of information (e.g., semistructured interview). If the rater were asked to complete a comprehensive scale on a frequent basis, time efficiency could be an issue; however, behavior rating scales tend not to be used in a formative manner. In addition, although the indirect nature of the scales increases the degree of inference needed in interpretation, intrusiveness on the environment is limited. Overall, when selecting a scale, feasibility must be considered with regard to the burden on existing resources.

Assistance with Assessment of Low-Frequency Behaviors

When a problem behavior occurs infrequently, direct assessment tools that require the presence of an outside individual can be problematic. If a behavior occurs only a few times a week, an external observer is unlikely to "catch" the behavior unless some information is available about when it is predicted to occur. Because the rater is asked to consider a larger time period (e.g., 1 month) when completing a behavior rating scale, the occurrence of low-frequency behaviors may be documented.

WHAT ARE THE WEAKNESSES ASSOCIATED WITH BEHAVIOR RATING SCALES?

Limited Evidence of Use in Progress Monitoring

As previously noted, evidence supporting the use of behavior rating scales in short-term progress monitoring is limited, and current recommendations are based on practical suggestions rather than empirical support. Most behavior rating scales are not designed to be sensitive to incremental change in behavior. Thus, their use is limited to long-term monitoring, such as in an evaluative capacity. However, when they are used in a pretest–posttest fashion, the effects of the intervention are not monitored directly, so linking behavior change to the intervention becomes difficult. Any number of factors could have affected behavioral change, including other interventions, changes in outside conditions (e.g., medications, family), different social relationships, or changes in instructional curriculum. Additionally, data obtained in a summative rather than formative manner reduces the opportunity to alter the intervention in a timely manner if it is not found to be effective.

Limited Use in Intraindividual Comparison

Behavior rating scale information is based on interindividual comparisons, that is, with a normative sample representing a larger population of students (usually national). Although useful for some purposes, such information limits our ability to understand the immediate context and behavior of an individual student and the specific effects of an intervention on behavior change. From one setting to the next, different expectations affect what is perceived as constituting appropriate behavior across different environments (e.g., classroom vs. playground, elementary vs. high school, rural vs. urban). Thus comparing a student's behavior to his or her own behavior and/or the behavior of local peers may be more relevant and informative.

Influence of the Rater

Perhaps the most significant weakness of this method is that the data are influenced by the perception of the rater rather than solely dependent on what is actually observed. Therefore, any noted change in ratings must first be considered as a possible change in the perception of the rater. Although a change in the student's behavior would be one reason for a change in rater perception, other possibilities should be considered (e.g., familiar vs. unfamiliar rater, good or bad previous experiences, limited fluency with the scale). In the end, if the need is to directly and objectively measure a student's behavior, behavior rating scales should be set aside in favor of other more direct methods. This is not, of course, to say that the perception of an adult is a categorically bad source of information; rather, this information source does not easily determine whether an intervention has actually changed a student's behavior.

Potential Cost

In contrast to methods requiring only paper and pencil, published norm-referenced behavior rating scales cost money to use. Although the individual protocols are not excessively expensive, the expense rises when they are used with a large number of students. In particular, the initial expenses associated with obtaining scoring sheets, training, manuals, and so forth can be high.

Focus on Problems Rather Than Strengths

Although comprehensive scales often include assessment of adaptive behavior, most behavior rating scales are focused on maladaptive behaviors and clinical problems. This emphasis can lead to excessive focus on what is wrong with the student rather than what the student does well, and can also potentially draw attention away from what can be done within a given context to support prosocial behavior.

CONCLUDING COMMENTS

In summary, behavior ratings scales should be considered indirect behavioral assessment tools. They involve rater perceptions about behavior, usually after the behavior has occurred. Obtained information should be considered a general estimate of behavior over time in comparison to a normative sample. Given these characteristics, comprehensive behavior rating scales are best suited for use in diagnostic and evaluative assessment to provide information about a broad range of behavioral constructs. Behavior rating scales are useful when progress toward short-term goals is being assessed or when the emphasis is on interindividual rather than intraindividual comparison. An increasing number of shorter behavior rating scales are being developed to focus on a specific range of behavior for use in progress monitoring. Evidence supporting this use is beginning to emerge. In conclusion, if a reliable estimate of a student's behavior in comparison to others is needed, then behavior rating scales might be a good choice. In terms of reliability, they can provide highly defensible estimates of a student's behavior across multiple dimensions. Such information can be useful in the development of behavioral interventions (Nelson et al., 2002), as well as the monitoring of longer-term goals. Given the relatively large amount of empirical attention directed toward the use of these tools, specific recommendations regarding their use will be available in the near future.

WHY *

7

Putting It All Together
Selecting Behavioral Assessment Tools

The majority of the chapters in the book review specific categories of behavioral assessment tools, including extant data, systematic direct observation (SDO), direct behavior ratings, and behavior rating scales. Although knowledge and skill regarding specific tools is necessary, it is not sufficient. As was emphasized in Chapter 1, the process of assessment must involve more than selecting and using a particular assessment tool. Assessment practices require effective and efficient collection and use of data to inform intervention and instruction—that is, to identify and solve a problem. In this chapter, we return to the guiding questions of why and which data are needed to illustrate how behavioral assessment tools can be appropriately selected for a particular situation. How those decisions might be made is illustrated through use of multiple case examples in which those decisions are embedded.

SELECTING BEHAVIORAL ASSESSMENT TOOLS: RETURNING TO THE GUIDING QUESTIONS

Although common characteristics exist across behavioral assessment tools, each tool is not equally suited for all assessment situations. And in many cases, more than one tool may be needed and/or be an appropriate choice. Thus guiding questions can facilitate decisions about assessment tools. As repeated throughout the book, those questions should first answer why the data are needed, and then which data are needed.

Why Do You Need the Data?

The first consideration when selecting an assessment tool is to ask why data are needed. Most often, this involves answering the question "What is the problem?" "Problems" in schools can range widely, from evaluation of the effectiveness of an after-school program in order to support continued funding of the program to a need to modify challenging behavior of a particular student. Good upfront problem identification facilitates an efficient assessment process in that efforts are not spent collecting data that are not needed in solving that problem. For example, a teacher reports difficulty managing student behavior. Further exploration of the problem behavior suggests that it relates to verbal aggression toward peers on the part of a small group of students during recess. This probing to define the problem situation gives us information about the definition of the problem behavior and the setting in which it is most likely to occur. Now we know that data need to be collected to assess the problem occurrence (e.g., frequency, intensity), which then guides decisions regarding intervention. In this example, answering why data are needed (i.e., to tell us about verbal aggression during recess) informs us about which data are needed. Rather than randomly collecting data that may not be relevant to the problem at hand or reason for assessment, assessment practices can become more efficient in providing what is needed to solve the problem. As previously noted, a wide variety of problems can be encountered in schools, such as those involving academic and/or social behavior of individuals or groups of students. Thus determining why assessment data are needed involves not only problem identification but also clarification of the reason for conducting the assessment (i.e., evaluation, screening, diagnosis, progress monitoring) as well as specification of the appropriate target level for assessment (universal, secondary, tertiary). We return to review of the four main reasons for engaging in assessment, but here we begin to connect assessment tools with those purposes.

First, the goal of *evaluation* is to provide a global, summative picture of behavior. Extant data, such as the results of statewide testing or quarterly grades, can be useful in evaluating behavior, particularly at the whole-school level, because they are readily available and collected on a large number of, if not all, students. Such data can be useful in painting a global, summative picture of a whole school, classroom, or even the individual student. Although indirect measures such as behavior rating scales provide an estimate of behavior over time for individual students, they may be best suited for secondary or tertiary (small group or individual student) situations given the associated time to complete and potential cost. Discrete snapshots of behavior provided through direct methods such as SDO are not as useful in evaluative purposes unless data can be easily aggregated. In addition, collection of multiple data points can be resource intensive, thus decreasing the efficiency of this tool in evaluative assessment. Although direct behavior ratings (DBRs) may be less resource intensive, derived data may not provide a complete evaluative picture because the ratings are intended to provide a snapshot of behavior in a particular period. And, given that the data are used to evaluate, often in a pretest–posttest fashion, it is important that the selected tools have established standards and provide meaningful information when summarized.

When data are needed to identify those students who are at risk, the assessment purpose involves *screening*. In such cases, an entire population or smaller subset is typically assessed, and further assessment and/or instructional and intervention efforts can then be directed toward those students whose behavior is discrepant. An efficient and effective screening tool generally does not provide specific detailed information about the student's behavior, as screening is meant to serve as an indicator of an underlying problem. Therefore, given potentially high costs and efforts, assessment tools such as SDO or comprehensive behavior rating scales are less likely to be used for screening purposes. In the case of direct observation, data provide an estimate of behavior in a given situation, which does not easily translate into a general indicator of overall student behavior. In contrast, comprehensive behavior rating scales can provide a general, global estimate of behavior—but the associated information can provide more detail than what is needed for screening. Thus in assessment situations involving screening, useful choices may include briefer versions of behavior rating scales, DBRs, or strategies that use extant data, such as curriculum-based measurement (CBM).

The goal in *diagnostic* assessment is to provide specific, comprehensive information about student behavior, such as identification of relevant skill assets and deficits. Such detailed information about a student's strengths and weaknesses can greatly assist in the process of intervention selection and development. For diagnostic purposes, virtually all assessment tools might be helpful in providing relevant information. For example, SDO and DBRs may be useful in determining and prioritizing the severity of the problem behavior in specific settings for intervention development. Behavior rating scales and extant data, particularly work samples, can be highly useful in diagnosing the specific behaviors and skills (or subskills) already falling within a student's repertoire and those that need further instructional effort. Given the potential appropriateness of most behavioral assessment tools in diagnostic assessment, selection becomes highly dependent on identification of the problem behavior. And, as is probably obvious, diagnostic assessment is typically engaged in at the individual or small-group level rather than universally or schoolwide.

Progress monitoring assessment is conducted with tools that allow for repeated evaluation over time. In the above example regarding problem behavior during recess, the reason for engaging in assessment is to develop an intervention for the problem behavior and then monitor change in behavior as a result of that intervention. Thus, the type of assessment is progress monitoring. Comprehensive behavior rating scales are generally not designed to be administered on a frequent repeated basis, particularly with large numbers of students. Progress monitoring data may be more appropriately collected through SDO or DBRs. However, selecting a particular tool for progress monitoring requires additional considerations, particularly as related to the efficiency and feasibility with which the data can be collected. For example, SDO may not be a good choice in situations in which (1) data must be collected frequently (e.g., once or many times a day) on multiple students, (2) behaviors are not considered serious (e.g., singing during instruction) and thus are "low stakes," or (3) many different and high-frequency behaviors are occurring. In these situations, DBRs or extant data that is regularly collected in a standardized fashion (e.g., attendance data) may be useful options given the potential increased efficiency.

In summary, the first step in an effective and efficient assessment process involves understanding why data are needed. In addition to identification of the problem behavior, this understanding involves simultaneous consideration of the level at which the problem should be solved (primary, secondary, tertiary) as well as the purpose for engaging in the assessment (i.e. evaluation, screening, diagnosis, program monitoring). Armed with these answers, it is possible to move to consideration of which data are needed.

Which Data Do I Need?

Answering the guiding question of which data are needed can be facilitated through consideration of three additional questions. Those questions include:

1. Which tools are best matched to assess the behavior of interest?
2. What decisions will be made using these data?
3. What resources are available to collect the data?

Although the questions are interrelated in determining which data are needed, each provides an additional unique contribution in an assessment process that is both *effective* and *efficient*. Further explanation of each is provided next.

Which Tools Are Best Matched to Assess the Behavior of Interest?

Answering this question involves determining which tools can provide meaningful and relevant information about the behavior of interest. For example, if tardiness was identified as the only behavior of interest, a comprehensive behavior rating scale would probably not be used unless it contained a high number of attendance-related items. Likewise, SDO would be a poor choice because recording would be limited to noting if a child was absent and/or came in late. In this example, attendance data would provide sufficient information about tardy behavior (e.g., frequency, day/setting).

When considering the "goodness of fit" between assessment tool and behavior of interest, *flexibility* and *frequency* should be examined. *Flexibility* refers to the degree to which the tool can be modified to fit the needs of an individual situation. For example, SDO and DBRs are highly customizable in terms of matching the target behaviors and data collection system (i.e., event- or time-based recording technique). In contrast, behavior rating scales are generally not as flexible. That is, although a behavior rating scale might be available that includes items of interest regarding the target behavior, those items are difficult to customize without compromise to the norm-referenced interpretation of the results. Likewise, although extant data might be selected that appropriately assess the target behavior, such data may not be easily adapted without significant change or burden to the existing system. Some assessment situations do not require that the tools be flexible. For example, extant schoolwide data such as attendance records are an appropriate choice for assessing the effectiveness of an intervention designed to increase attendance, despite the tool's "inflexibility" with regard to modification. In the end, flexibility of a tool is an advantage only if one needs to adapt the observation method to fit the behavior of interest.

The second consideration relates to the *frequency* with which data collection is desired. A general rule of thumb is "the more outcome data, the better for decision making." Although a behavior rating scale might address an initial screening and/or final evaluation assessment of the target behavior, these tools are generally inappropriate for daily administration, such as when monitoring incremental change in behavior. If data are needed on a frequent basis (e.g., daily, weekly), extant data, direct observation, or DBRs are more appropriate tools. However, as discussed under the third question, some of these tools are more resource intensive than others. Thus selection of an appropriate tool involves balancing the value of having a certain type and volume of data against the costs associated with collecting those data.

What Decisions Will Be Made Using These Data?

A second guiding question with regard to which data are needed relates to the type of decisions to be made. Types of educational decisions are often discussed in terms of "low stakes" versus "high stakes." Low-stakes decisions are common, everyday decisions (e.g., change in instruction, moving up or down within a curriculum) that are not intended to impact the student in irreversible ways. These decisions guide ongoing classroom management and instruction. In contrast, high-stakes decisions are those that have the potential to significantly impact the student for long periods of time (e.g., out-of-school placement, special education). One of the more important and serious high-stakes decisions is the labeling of a student as disabled, and good data are essential to supporting such decisions. Because lower-stakes decisions are being made on a regular basis, the degree of precision may be less important than feasibility, and thus less direct data sources might be selected. However, when the stakes are high, data errors can lead to decisions with serious negative outcomes. Because room for error is small, multiple sources of data must be used to confirm and validate interpretation and associated decisions about instruction and intervention. For example, although a behavior rating scale may be highly reliable, valid, and based on a representative norm sample, a high-stakes decision should not be made with a single rating scale due to the indirect nature of the information. In particular, interpretation of behavior rating scale data is mediated by a number of factors, such as rater influence and separation of data collection from the time in which the behavior actually occurred.

However, this does not mean that indirect tools such as behavior rating scales should not be used in a high-stakes decision. Although general recommendations are to use measures that are direct as possible, it is important to understand the limitations of directness as well. That is, the more direct the tool, the less reliable that data will be in describing behavior over time (e.g., the less likely it is that similar results will be found at different times). For example, SDO data basically provide a snapshot of what behavior is occurring during the specified observation period. Although the student might be prone to aggressive behavior, whether the student displays the aggressive behavior can vary, for example, by time and setting. Observational data taken during periods in which aggressive behavior is not displayed would not be accurate in providing a complete picture of this student's behavior. Thus, although highly direct measures are important for estimating behavior during a specific time, setting, and activity, these tools are not as well suited for making general statements about child behavior across times, settings, or activities. And sometimes, these general statements are necessary when making high-stakes decisions. So, indirect tools such as behavior rating scales, which are designed to have the rater consider a larger sample of the target child's behavior, can lead to information that is generalizable to a greater range of contexts. In the end, educators must consider the situation at hand and ask if highly direct or highly generalizable information is most important, or if both might be needed.

What Resources Are Available to Collect the Data?

The final consideration guiding decisions about what data are needed relates to *practicality*. Although it is necessary to understand the technical characteristics of an assessment tool, the feasibility of using that tool with fidelity is equally important. No matter how perfect an assessment plan may seem, it will likely fail if the resources needed for implementation are not reasonable for the situation.

Recognizing feasibility of an assessment tool starts with determining the resources that are available to collect the data. For example, who will be responsible for administration, summary, and interpretation? In situations where the classroom teacher or other support staff collect assessment data, tools such as extant data probably are least intrusive on daily routines because information is already being collected and can later be examined in detail at a more convenient time and place. DBRs may also be considered highly feasible because only a few seconds are needed to indicate a rating based on the behavior that was previously observed. In situations in which a person other than a classroom teacher collects data, more resource-intensive tools such as SDO can be considered, especially when collecting multiple data points. Simply because a tool is more feasible does not mean that it always should be used. As previously noted, the type of decision to be made (high stakes, low stakes) can be a relevant factor. However, given the limited resources generally prevalent in applied settings like schools, it is likely that more feasible yet appropriate tools will be desirable.

Four aspects of resource feasibility might be considered. Those aspects include time needed for implementation, amount of training to achieve accurate use, intrusiveness on the environment, and financial cost for obtaining and using the tool. Each of these dimensions should be considered within the context of the level of and reason for assessment (why data are needed). For example, behavior rating scales require little training on the part of the rater but significant training for the person responsible for interpreting the results. Behavior rating scales are generally feasible for diagnostic uses at the tertiary level in terms of cost, time, and intrusiveness, as the time required to complete one is limited to a single occasion and it can be completed at the convenience of the rater. However, use of comprehensive behavior rating scales for diagnosis at the primary level (e.g., the entire first grade) may not represent an efficient use of time or money. In that situation, assessments using extant data may be more resource feasible. Assuming that extant data are readily available and efficiently, consistently, and accurately collected and summarized, then training time, costs, and intrusiveness can be minimal. Likewise, DBRs require relatively minimal training for the rater and are comparatively low in cost; however, intrusiveness can be slightly greater than with extant data because the rater must integrate behavior rating and scoring into the immediate routines of the classroom or setting.

The implications of intrusiveness cannot be overlooked when creating an assessment plan. Intrusiveness is most often a concern with respect to disrupting typical classroom routines and activities. Assessment involving extant data is minimally intrusive compared to behavior rating scales, SDO, and direct behavior ratings. For example, SDO data collected in the classroom can be highly intrusive during the activities of both teachers and students. Presence of a new, outside observer also can have a reactive effect on student and teacher behavior (e.g., "He stopped doing that as soon as you walked in the class-

TABLE 7.1. Examining the Categories of Behavior Assessment Tools with Regard to Progress Monitoring

Guiding question	Permanent products	Behavior rating scales	Direct observation	Direct behavior ratings
At what level do I need *progress monitoring* data?				
• Primary	Probably	Maybe	Maybe	Maybe
• Secondary	Probably	Maybe	Probably	Probably
• Tertiary	Probably	Maybe	Probably	Probably
What decisions will be made using these *progress monitoring* data?				
• High stakes	Maybe	Probably	Probably	Maybe
• Low stakes	Probably	Maybe	Probably	Probably
Which tools are best matched to *monitor the progress* of behavior of interest?				
• Frequency	High	Low	High	High
• Flexibility	Medium	Low	High	High
What resources are available to collect the *progress monitoring* data?				
• Time	Low	High	High	Medium
• Training	Low	Low	High	Low
• Intrusiveness	Low	Low	High	Medium
• Cost	Low	Medium/high	Low	Low

Note. Ask yourself whether the tool is appropriate for use with regard to the categories listed within each guiding question.

room!"). Degree of intrusiveness can even vary within a category of assessment tool. For example, a specific-type rating scale comprising 10 items is less intrusive with respect to teacher time and effort than a comprehensive scale with 110 items.

Because answering each guiding question reciprocally informs the answer to the others, definitively stating that a particular tool is good for one purpose but not another is difficult to do. Beginning with the level of and reason for assessment (Why do you need data?), selection choices can be narrowed; however, all questions can be relevant prior to making final decisions about tools for each assessment situation. To illustrate how the categories of assessment might be compared, sample answers for the guiding questions with regard to *progress monitoring* are indicated in Table 7.1. Each type of assessment tool is rated as "probably" or "maybe" useful for each level and type of decision. Appropriateness for the behavior of interest and resources is listed as "low," "medium," and "high." Finally, because many assessment situations call for the use of multiple data sources, selecting a behavior assessment tool must not be considered an "all or none" process.

CASE EXAMPLES

To support and illustrate the use of guiding questions to select behavior assessment tools, three case studies are presented. In each, the rationale for answering the guiding questions is given.

Case Example: Chris

Recently, Chris has been exhibiting high levels of off-task behavior in Ms. Wilson's seventh-grade English class. Although Ms. Wilson does not describe this behavior as highly problematic at this time (not a high-stakes situation), the importance of addressing it before it becomes more significant is acknowledged. After consultation with the seventh-grade team of teachers working with Chris, a tentative intervention plan is discussed and data collection tools are considered. Ms. Wilson makes it clear that she is not interested in highly invasive, resource-intensive data collection strategies. Additionally, the 7th-grade team decides it would like information about how Chris's behavior compares to that of other students across settings. In this case, the presenting problem falls at the secondary at-risk level (individual student), and the reason for the assessment involves diagnosis as well as progress monitoring. The team uses Figure 7.1 to guide decisions regarding what data are needed. Because this situation is low stakes, and in consideration of Ms. Wilson's stated preferences, the team seeks to obtain assessment data with tools that require limited training, time, and intrusiveness. Thus, the following assessment tools are selected:

1. General-purpose behavior rating scale, completed by the core teachers.
2. DBRs of on-task behavior, completed daily by Ms. Wilson following her class period with Chris.

The behavior rating scale provides information about a variety of behaviors across settings. The scales involve low frequency (one-time completion) and low flexibility, since they are comprehensive and items cannot be modified. The DBRs are well matched to this specific referral problem in that the tools have (1) high flexibility (i.e., can be designed to specifically target attention problems) and (2) high frequency of use (e.g., completed daily at the end of class). Demands related to training and required time for completion are low, addressing many of Ms. Wilson's concerns.

Case Example: Susie, Sally, and Sandy

Susie, Sally, and Sandy have been exhibiting significant amounts of in-class verbal aggression (e.g., name calling, teasing) in Mr. Simon's class, and each student has been sent to the principal's office on numerous occasions. After consultation with the student services team, a secondary-level (i.e., common intervention for all three students deemed at risk) assessment and intervention plan is discussed, with emphasis on collecting data for progress monitoring. Three options are discussed:

1. Office discipline referrals (ODRs).
2. Systematic direct observation involving frequency count of instances of verbal aggression.
3. DBRs of prosocial behavior completed by teacher and/or student(s).

ODRs are useful because they are readily available and require minimal training and time. However, ODRs may not provide an accurate picture of the problem behavior, par-

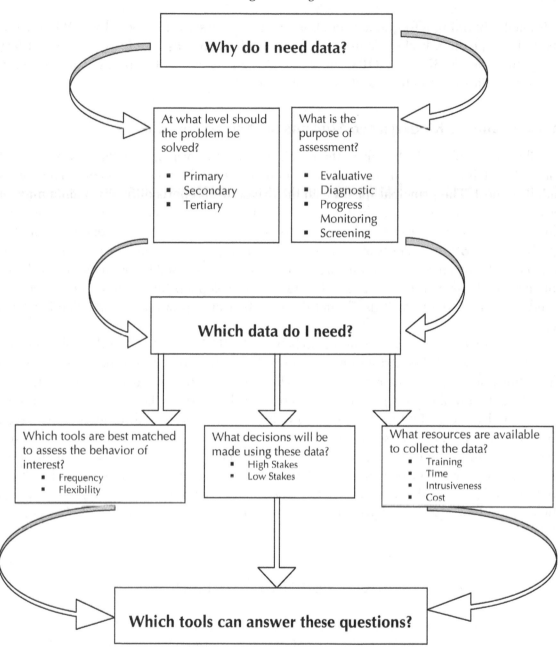

FIGURE 7.1. Questions that guide selection of a behavioral assessment tool.

ticularly if the observed verbal aggression is not severe enough to warrant office involvement. DBRs may be a better option for obtaining progress monitoring data. DBRs, particularly if used in self-monitoring of prosocial behavior (e.g., complimenting a classmate) could be useful, especially to assess behavior that could be missed by the teacher and to prompt and potentially reinforce engagement in prosocial behavior through the self-rating. DBRs can be well matched to a particular behavior of interest (high goodness of fit) because of their flexibility in use and minimal training and time requirements. Summarizing the DBR data can be made efficient by including it as part of the intervention.

Although obtaining a frequency count of verbally aggressive instances by SDO may initially be appealing, higher degrees of effort and intrusiveness are likely to make it less appealing than DBRs or ODRs, unless SDOs can be completed by external observer. Therefore, in this situation, SDO was not selected.

Case Example: Kindergarten Students at Pine Grove School

While reviewing ODR data from the past 3 months, the principal at Pine Grove School notices that Bus 7 has a disproportionate number of ODRs relating to compliance with adult request. The principal speaks with the driver, who reports difficulty maintaining an acceptable level of noise on the bus. Because "all" the students on his bus are much too loud and do not listen to him when asked to lower their voices, he has been handling the problem by writing students office referrals for disrespect/noncompliance. Both the principal and the bus driver agree this problem should be addressed before it escalates. Thus, the principal enlists the student services team to develop a primary intervention plan (all kindergarten students on Bus 7), and the selection of appropriate data collection tools ensues.

Although ODR data will continue to be useful, ODRs do not reflect the behavior that is less severe yet still contributing to the overall problem (e.g., the student speaking in a loud but not seriously distracting tone). The team asks the bus driver to use SDO by counting the number of reprimands given over each bus ride when students have excessively loud voices. SDO in this case allows for high flexibility and frequency. However, because intrusiveness of use is high, a golf counter is used to make data collection easier for the driver to manage, especially because another adult is not present on the bus. Once the intervention plan involving teaching expectations for bus behavior has been determined to be effective, use of the SDO is discontinued. ODR data continue to be reviewed on a periodic basis to ensure the intervention plan continues to be successful.

CONCLUDING COMMENTS

In a period of increased accountability, pressure to document the effectiveness of academic and social instruction and intervention has mounted. Decisions about students can no longer be made without defensible data supporting those decisions. An assessment process built on effectively and efficiently producing data to guide those decisions is clearly needed. Although many very good references exist on behavioral assessment, this book provides a comprehensive reference to tie information together as relevant to school settings. This includes consideration of both academic and social behavior across levels of focus and reasons for assessment. In this concluding chapter, we have drawn together the information presented in this book about our decision-making model for school-based behavioral assessment. In this model, guiding questions are used to drive the methods and practices used in assessment. The guiding questions of which data are needed and why facilitate effective and efficient assessment that can inform decisions about instruction and intervention. In Appendix 7.1, an organizer is provided to increase further the precision of instructional and intervention decisions related to data collection needs and uses. The importance of considering school-based behavioral assessment as a process for identifying and solving a problem cannot be overstated. As demonstrated through the examples provided throughout the book, although the problem varies across contexts, the guiding questions remain applicable.

NOTE

Portions of this chapter were adapted, with the permission of the California Association of School Psychologists, from Riley-Tillman, T. C., Kalberer, S. M., & Chafouleas, S. M. (2005). Selecting the right tool for the job: A review of behavior monitoring tools used to assess student response to intervention. *The California School Psychologist, 10,* 81–91.

QUESTION-BASED ORGANIZER FOR DATA COLLECTION NEEDS

Assessment question	Who needs the information?	When do they need the information?	What data need to be collected?	How and when will data be collected?
1.				
2.				
3.				
4.				
5.				

Appendix

Guidelines for Summarizing and Interpreting Behavioral Data

Although the process of making decisions about which data are needed and collecting those data constitutes a relatively large initial effort in behavioral assessment, the process is not complete without summary and interpretation. Thus, guidelines are given below to aid in the summary and interpretation of assessment data, especially formative assessment data used to monitor the effects of intervention implementation. For ease in demonstrating the summarization/analysis method and because they are likely to be used in school settings, simple AB intervention designs (baseline data followed by an intervention) are illustrated. Although a comprehensive review of other single-subject invention designs is beyond the scope of this book, please see Table A.1 for a brief overview.

SUMMARIZING DATA THROUGH VISUAL PRESENTATION: CREATING THE LINE GRAPH

Although data may be summarized in many ways, visual formats (vs. a table or just list of numbers) are the most effective and efficient (e.g., bar chart, scatterplot, line graph). In particular, line graphs provide a simple way to review data collected over time, especially for progress monitoring. Steps for summarizing data with line graphs follow:

1. Label the y (vertical) axis with behavior of interest (e.g., percentage of time on task or number of times a student calls out).
2. Select the scale for the y axis based on the data collected (e.g., 0% to 100% for percentage of time on task or percentage of intervals out of seat, number of words per minute, number of aggressive acts per day, average daily DBR rating).
3. Select the scale for and label the x (horizontal) axis with observation intervals (e.g., day, period, week).
4. Separate preintervention (baseline) and intervention phase data with a vertical dashed line (e.g., 5 days of baseline data followed by 15 days of intervention).
5. Connect consecutive data points within phases to show progress. To highlight summary of data within phases, do not connect lines across phases (i.e., preintervention to intervention), or across missing data. Represent missing data points by a break in lines and changes in intervention conditions with a vertical line.

TABLE A.1. Summary of Possible Intervention Designs

Name of design	Description	When you might want to use this design	Limitations to consider
AB	A baseline (no treatment phase) is followed by the introduction of an intervention. This is the most basic of all of the single-subject designs.	• When you are more concerned with simply finding a treatment that works rather than demonstrating experimental control	• Weak demonstration of experimental control (does not account for other possible factors influencing the dependent variable)
ABAB	After the intervention has been introduced, it is withdrawn to see whether the behavior reverses to baseline levels and then reintroduced to see if the effect of the intervention is replicated.	• When the behavior is reversible (and it is ethical to reverse it) • When the effects of the treatment on the behavior will significantly decrease (or disappear) once the treatment is removed	• Returning the behavior to baseline may be difficult or undesirable • Takes more time than a simple AB design
Multiple baseline	The basic AB design is replicated within the same investigation across at least three people, behaviors, or settings. Although all three baselines begin at the same time, introduction of the intervention is staggered across individuals, behaviors, or settings.	• When withdrawing the intervention, or reversing the effects of an intervention, is impossible or unethical • When intervention is needed for more than one individual, behavior, or setting	• Time and resources necessary • Must control for cross-baseline factors • Must ensure independence across baselines (they do not covary) • All individuals, behaviors, or settings must be expected to react in a similar way to one intervention
Alternating treatments	The relative effectiveness of different treatments is determined by rapidly alternating the introduction of counterbalanced treatments over time.	• When you want to compare multiple treatments quickly and efficiently • When the treatments are sufficiently different from one another • When behavior is severe enough to warrant skipping a baseline phase, *or* baseline data are unavailable or highly unstable (it is not necessary to collect baseline data in an alternating treatments design)	• The learner must be able to discriminate among treatments/conditions • Possible multiple treatment interference (treatments might interact) • Possible difficulty reversing effects • Ensuring implementation fidelity more difficult (counterbalancing interventions and ensuring they are introduced an equal number of times) • Not useful if treatment produces slow behavioral change
Changing criterion	A variation on the basic AB design in which the baseline phase (A) is followed by an intervention phase (B), which is divided into subphases. Within each subphase, the implementer establishes a response criterion level, waits for the behavior to reach the criterion level, and then establishes a new criterion (either increases or decreases).	• When the target behavior is likely to be responsive to contingency changes (and change gradually in a stepwise fashion) • When the student has demonstrated that he or she can perform the target behavior, but the behavior needs to be increased or decreased • When withdrawing the treatment is not appropriate or possible	• Time • Should be used only when the intervention is contingency-based (reinforcement/punishment) • Can be difficult to determine/set the criterion levels

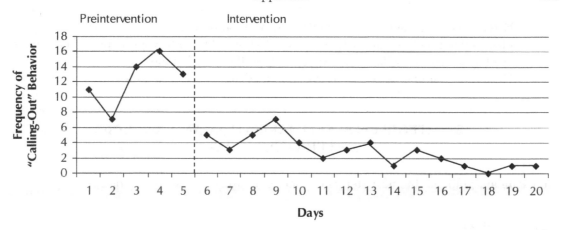

FIGURE A.1. Example sample intervention graph.

In Figure A.1, "calling-out" behavior (y axis) was recorded once a day for a total of 20 days (x axis). Visual analysis reveals that the maximum number of calling-out behaviors reported in a day is 16 (scale set at 0 to 18). (Note that the same scales should be used when comparing information across graphs in order to avoid inaccurate interpretation due to visual presentation.) The vertical dotted line separates the preintervention (baseline) period from the intervention phase and enables an evaluation of the effectiveness of an intervention. Consecutive data points within phases are connected.

Goal lines are useful for interpretation of intervention effectiveness (see Figure A.2), and are based on an intervention team's determination of where the behavior should be at the end of a specified period of time. This behavior goal is expressed on the graph using the following steps:

1. Find the median (middle value) of the last three baseline data points on the y axis.
2. Place a point on the graph where x = the last day of the baseline data, and y = the median value identified in Step 1.
3. Determine the desired level for the behavior at the end of the intervention period, as well as the length of the period.

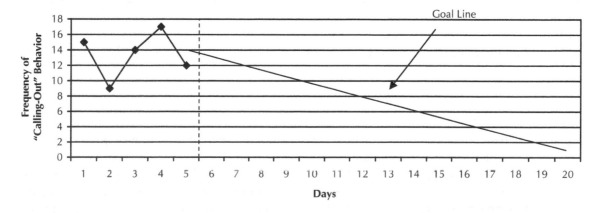

FIGURE A.2. Adding a goal line to the intervention phase.

4. Extend the x axis out over the entire intervention period.
5. Place a point on the graph where x = the last day of the intervention period and y = the level at which the behavior is expected to be if the goal is met.
6. Draw the goal line between the baseline median and the goal point.

STRATEGIES FOR SUMMARIZATION AND ANALYSIS OF BEHAVIORAL DATA

After data are graphed, the next step is to conduct a visual analysis of the data.

Visual Analysis

Visual analysis includes examining (1) change in mean, (2) change in level, (3) immediacy of change, and (4) variability in the data.

Change in Mean

The most basic way to interpret data is to compare the mean of the data during the baseline phase with the mean of the data in the intervention phase. In Figure A.1, the mean number of observed "calling-out" behavior in baseline was 12.2 times a day compared to 2.8 times per day during the intervention phase. Although an analysis of means suggests a dramatic decrease, examining intervention effectiveness using only means provides an incomplete conclusion. In the example, not only is there a decrease in rate of talkouts between phases, but during the intervention phase the rate of talkouts is a decreasing trend. Another concern is the impact of single deviant data point on the mean. In the example, if data for days 14 and 15 were actually 1 and 3, instead of 17 and 22, respectively, the intervention mean would increase from 2.8 to 5.1. Thus, mean scores should be considered in the context of whether they occur within and between phase trends.

Change in Level

Visual analysis also involves an examination of data immediately after intervention is initiated, referred to as level or step changes. In Figure A.3, the arrow indicates the point at which there is a large change in the level of the rate of behavior. A large and immediate change in level between baseline and intervention phases is desirable, as is mentioned in the next paragraph discussing latency of change. If no change in level is noted between phases, possible changes in trend at the time of intervention should be examined. Level changes within a phase might indicate the influence of a factor external to the intervention or instruction (either facilitating or interfering).

Latency of Change

Latency of change refers to amount of time for the intervention to have an impact on the behavior. Intervention effects can be immediate or delayed, thus examination of behavior trends will be important to include in the analysis of latency of change, that is, the closer in time the observed change is to the initiation of the intervention, the greater the likelihood that the behavior change is related to the intervention. An analysis of baseline and intervention data represented in Figure A.4 suggests that the impact of the intervention is immediate.

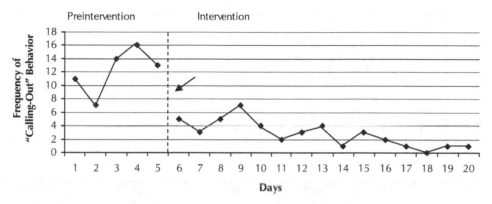

FIGURE A.3. Examination of change in level from baseline to intervention.

Variability

Variability refers to the amount of variation in range and/or consistency in a set of data. In Figure A.5, a classwide intervention was implemented to decrease "out-of-seat" behavior. In the baseline phase, considerable variability can be observed. (Note: mean scores would not be representative.) However, during intervention, overall level and variability of problem behavior are decreased.

Percentage of Nonoverlapping Data

The percentage of nonoverlapping data points (PND) is calculated to examine the degree of variability, that is, "how much does the behavior at the time of the intervention look like the behavior prior to the intervention?" or "what percentage of the data during the intervention does not overlap with data during the baseline phase?" When calculating PND, the first consideration is determining the expected change in direction. In the example presented in Figure A.4, behavior is expected to increase as a result of the intervention. To compute the PND, the number of intervention data points falling above the highest baseline data point (in this case, 14) is determined and

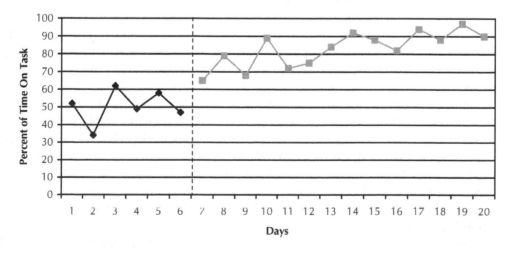

FIGURE A.4. Examination of latency of change across baseline and intervention phases.

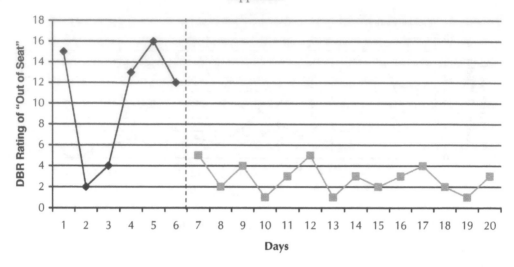

FIGURE A.5. Example intervention graph demonstrating high variability in baseline with decreased variability during intervention.

divided by the total number of intervention data points (in this case, 14). The result (14/14, or 100% nonoverlapping data) suggests that the behavior is different (in the right direction!) in comparison to data collected in the baseline phase. Although the intervention in Figure A.5 was considered effective, the significant amount of variability during baseline results in a low percentage of nonoverlapping data points. Specifically, only 3 of 14 intervention observations (about 21%) do not overlap with baseline data. Thus, when data are highly variable, PND in isolation can fail to identify an effective intervention.

Change in Trend

Change in trend is another important consideration in visual analysis. A simple method for determining trend (i.e., celeration) is the split-middle technique (White, as cited in Kazdin, 1982), which is applied to datasets within phases. The steps for determining a split-middle trend line for each phase are as follows (see Figure A.6):

1. Split data within a phase in half. In the example, the baseline data are split into two groups of 3 points, and the intervention phase data are split into two groups of 7 points. If working with an odd number of data points, make the split at the middle data point (i.e., point 3 of 5), and do not include this point in the remaining steps.
2. Within each half of each phase, identify the point where the middle value on the x axis meets the middle value on the y axis. On the x axis, the median value will always be the middle day or session. On the y axis, the median value is identified. For example, in Figure A.6, the middle day in the first half of baseline data would be the second day (the median of 1, 2, and 3) on the x axis (days) and the third data point (which is 50, or the median of 35, 50, and 54) on the y axis (percent of time on task). A line is drawn vertically through the x axis median and horizontally through the y axis median point so an intersection is indicated.
3. Connect the two points formed by the median values for each half to form the trend line

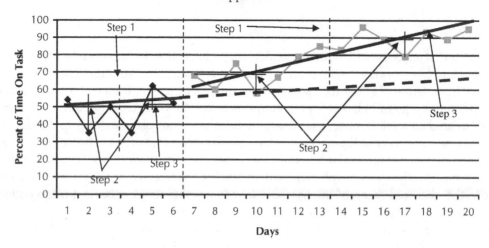

FIGURE A.6. Step-by-step procedures for using the split-middle technique.

for those data of that phase. The same procedure is applied to the intervention data to determine a second trend line.

4. Describe the trend lines within and between phases with respect to direction and change. By extending the trend line beyond the data used to draw the initial line, a tentative prediction of future behavior is indicated and can be used to analyze current behavior patterns (e.g., intervention effects vs. predicted performance if baseline had been continued).

The data in Figure A.6 might be described as follows: During baseline a slightly accelerating trend was indicated with moderate variability. After intervention was initiated on Day 6, a small initial upward level change was observed and a slight increase in accelerating trend was indicated with no change in variability. By comparing the intervention trend line to a projected baseline trend, the effect of the intervention is determined to be positive because the on-task behavior increased or accelerated once the intervention was implemented.

Celeration lines can be used to visualize goal development and decision making by following these steps:

1. Identify the points on the celeration line corresponding to the first and last day of the phase (e.g., Days 1 and 6 in baseline) and determine the y values (percent of time on task). On Day 1 in the example, the celeration line is at 50% of time on task. On Day 5, the celeration line is at 52% of time on task. In the intervention phase, on Day 14 the celeration line is at 83%, and 93% four days later (Day 18).

2. Divide the larger value by the smaller value. In this case, 52/50 results in 1.04, which means that during baseline, the percentage of time on task increased 0.04% over the course of 5 days, which would be a long time before substantial change might be realized. In the intervention phase, on the other hand, 93/83 results in 1.12, indicating an increase of 12% over the same period of 5 days.

Computing behavioral change numerically can be beneficial in determining the length of time before a goal will be reached. In the current example, to achieve the goal of a 40% gain in on-task behavior, 100 school weeks with no intervention in place would have been required. With the intervention that goal was obtained in less than 3 weeks.

Effect Sizes

A final method of analysis, which involves calculating effect sizes, has become increasingly important as demand has grown for quantitative evidence to justify intervention choices (see Thompson, 2006). Calculation of effect size demonstrates the practical significance of intervention results by quantifying change in behavior in a uniform manner. The most common form of effect size is the standardized mean difference, the change in mean from the baseline phase to the intervention phase expressed in terms of the observed standard deviation (*SD*). (Note: It can be important to understand how the *SD* is standardized when interpreting data.) Effect sizes are presented in *SD* units, so that a 1.0 effect size simply tells us that the observed mean of the intervention data is one *SD* above the observed mean of the baseline data. Given this standardization, intervention comparisons can be made quickly across students, settings, and even studies.

Several methods are available for calculating effect size depending on the selected standard deviation. The following method of calculating standardized mean difference is easy and makes no assumptions about the distributions of scores (Daly, Chafouleas, & Skinner, 2005). The formula (Busk & Serlin, 1992) is as follows:

$$\frac{\text{(Mean of Intervention Phase} - \text{Mean of Baseline Phase)}}{\text{Standard Deviation of Baseline Phase}}$$

The following information is needed to compute the effect size:

1. Mean of the data in the baseline phase
2. Standard deviation of the data in the baseline phase
3. Mean of the data in the intervention phase

Using the example in Figure A.4, the mean in the baseline phase is 50.57, the *SD* in the baseline phase is 8.94, and the mean in the intervention phase is 83.87. Thus, in this example, the effect size is:

$$\frac{80.85 - 50.57}{8.94} = 3.4$$

The effect size of 3.4 indicates that the intervention mean was 3.4 *SD* above the observed baseline mean, suggesting that the intervention was highly effective. Suggested guidelines for interpretation of effect sizes have been presented as "rules of thumb." For example, Cohen (1988) speculated that an effect size of 0.20 should be considered small, 0.50 is moderate, and 0.80 or above is large. Empirical examination of these "rules of thumb" was conducted by Lipsey (1990), who found an effect size of 0.15 to be small, 0.45 to be moderate, and 0.90 to be large. Although these guidelines can provide a general sense of effect size interpretation, the guidelines are not perfect, as they were taken across a number of contexts and outcomes in the social sciences (Bloom, Hill, Black, & Lipsey, 2006). Bloom and colleagues have stressed the importance of using a frame of reference appropriate to the context (e.g., outcome being measured, intervention being studied, samples being examined) in interpreting the magnitude of effect sizes. For example, given the expectation of greater growth in reading skills during the elementary years, larger effect sizes would be expected for elementary reading skills versus high school reading skills; however, smaller effect sizes found in high school do not necessarily mean that the intervention was less effective.

In summary, a number of options exist for the summarization and analysis of assessment data. Generally, a combination of strategies is utilized rather than a single method. Computer-based technologies are widely available to assist with the calculations in summary and interpretation. For example, "Chart Dog" (found free at *www.interventioncentral.org*) offers support for graphing data and computing (1) the mean value in a phase, (2) PND by phase, (3) a trend line for a data series, and (4) effect size for any treatment phase when compared to a baseline phase.

MOVING FROM SUMMARIZATION AND ANALYSIS TO DECISION MAKING

After data are summarized and described, decisions related to a number of questions can be made, for example, "Is the intervention working?" "Should we change the intervention?" or "Do we need a new intervention?"

Before directly addressing a question, the first step when interpreting data within the context of the assessment situation is to determine whether the data are adequate to answer the questions. Adequacy is determined by considering questions such as what data should be and have been collected, what method was used to collect the data, and whether the method was used appropriately. Additional questions to ask regarding your data are presented in Table A.2 (adapted from Merrell, 2003).

If the collected data can appropriately answer the intended questions, interpretation of the data patterns can occur at two levels. First, the intervention process should be one in which effective decisions can be made. In Figure A.7, a step-by-step process for an effective intervention process is provided.

Effective monitoring of intervention effects also requires more specific decisions. In Table A.3, types of decisions that can be made based on data analysis are presented, and data interpretation ("If . . ." column) corresponds to intervention action plan ("Then . . ." column). In the example involving "out-of-seat" behavior (see Figure A.5), analysis of the data suggests a decrease in that behavior. If agreement is reached that the goal has been met, a decision can be made to (1) continue the intervention as is, (2) discontinue the intervention outright, or (3) institute procedures to fade the use of the intervention. In this case, for example, a decision could involve continuing the intervention but changing the target behavior to another of interest. Given this decision, a phase line is drawn, a new goal or goal date is established, and data collection and monitoring continues.

To provide additional guidance in decision making, the *3-point decision rule* can be applied. Using the 3-point decision rule, the last three intervention data points are examined to determine if they fall (1) well below (deceleration target) or above (acceleration target) the goal line (good

---

TABLE A.2. Questions to Ask When Interpreting Your Data

- Do the data confirm the identified problem?
- What additional information do the data provide?
- How can we use the data to answer the referral questions?
- Are there other factors that appear to be contributing to the problem?
- Are any data missing (and if so, how will I collect those data)?

Note. Based on Merrell (2003).

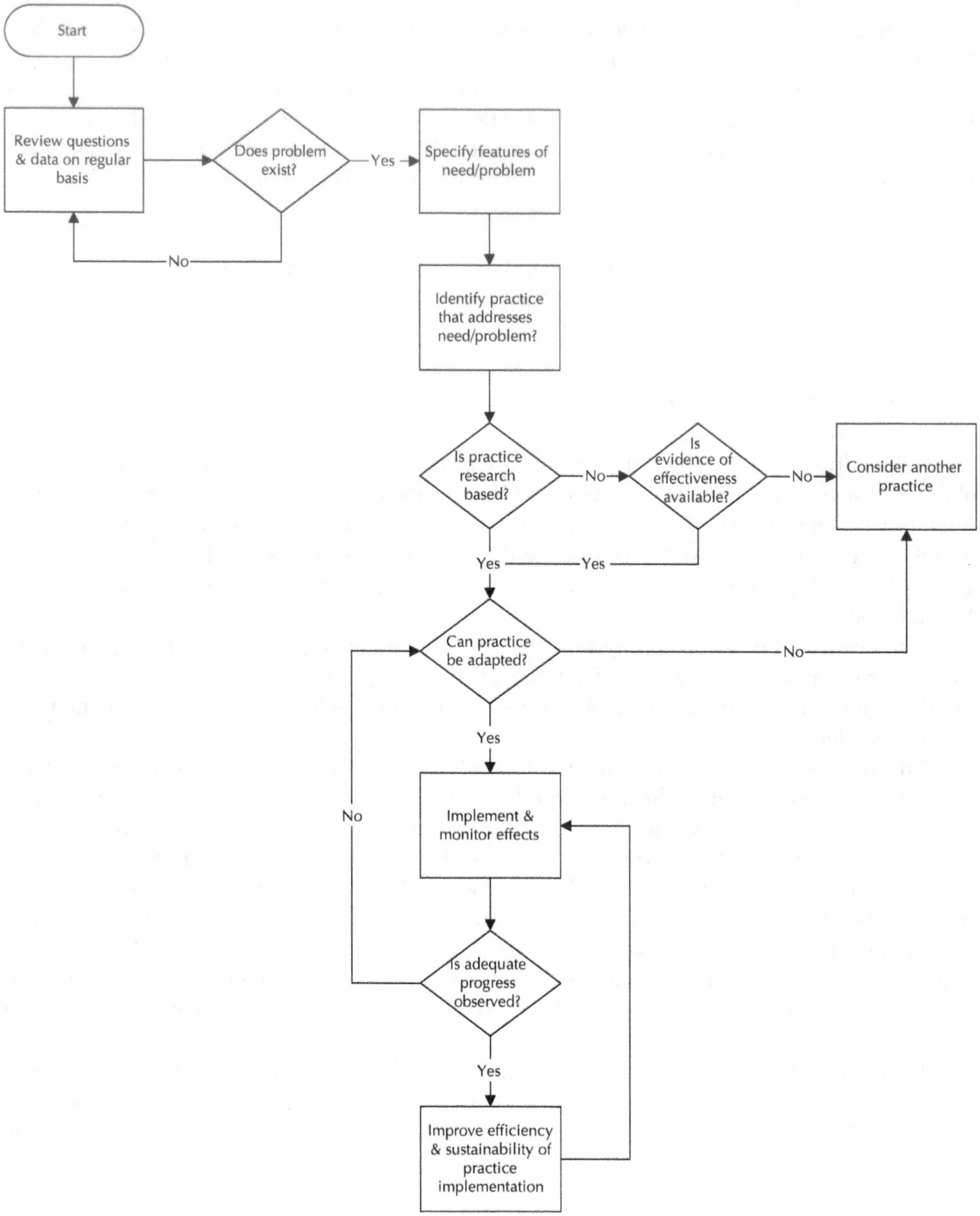

FIGURE A.7. Suggested process for intervention decision making.

progress) or (2) around the goal line (adequate progress toward goal). If good progress is being made, decisions might be made to modify the intervention for efficiency and maintenance of effects. In Figure A.8, examples of the use of the 3-point decision rule are presented. The solid line represents the goal, and a decrease in behavior is desired. The pattern in the top line of intervention data does not suggest that the goal will be attained in the time allotted; thus, a change to the intervention should be considered. The middle line of data appears to fall around the goal line, which suggests that the goal is likely to be met in the time allotted, and that the intervention should continue as planned. Finally, the bottom line of intervention data suggests that the goal will be attained more quickly than expected, and that perhaps some changes to the intervention could be considered.

TABLE A.3. Possible Intervention Decisions Based on Collected Data

If . . .	Then . . .	Description
The student is making sufficient progress toward a goal,	Make no change.	Continue to monitor progress, but make no changes to the current intervention program.
It does not look like the student will achieve his or her goal in the allotted amount of time, but you feel that the intervention is appropriate and is having positive effects,	Change the goal date.	Push back the date by which you expect the student to achieve the goal.
The student has been successful with some part of the behavior/skill but is not making progress overall,	Slice back.	Slice back the behavior/skill to a more manageable level. For academic behaviors, perhaps focus on only one type of problem at a time. For social behaviors, perhaps reduce the behavioral goal (e.g., aim for 60% on task rather than 80%).
The current work is simply too difficult for the student to be successful,	Step back.	Step back to teach and review an earlier skill in order to ensure that the student possesses the prerequisite skills.
You believe the goal that is in place is appropriate for the student, but he or she is not making sufficient progress,	Try a different instructional procedure.	Make a change to either the antecedent conditions (e.g., try a different method of teaching a skill in the case of academic behavior) or consequent conditions (e.g., ignore problem behaviors rather than reprimanding the student in the case of social behavior).
The student's progress seems to have reached a sufficient plateau (started off progressing at an adequate rate but then flattened out or dropped off at 80%),	Move on to a new phase of learning.	Although the student is performing the behavior accurately, he or she may now need to work on building fluency. It may be necessary to provide more time to practice the skill or additional incentives for improving fluency.
The student has met his or her goal more quickly than expected (and the behavior is observed across settings to be both accurate and fluent),	Move on to a new skill.	Establish a new goal for the student. This could be accomplished by either setting a higher goal for the same behavior or moving on to an entirely new skill/ behavior.
You believe the goal that is in place is appropriate for the student and he or she is already receiving adequate assistance to meet the goal but is not making progress,	Begin compliance training.	It may be necessary to work on improving the student's responsiveness to teacher directives.

Note. Based in part on Wolery et al. (1988).

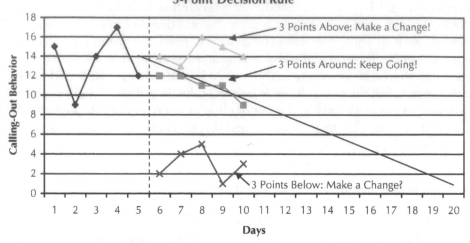

FIGURE A.8. Using the 3-point decision rule to make intervention decisions.

CONCLUDING COMMENTS

In summary, many options for summarization and analysis of behavioral data exist, and typically options are used in combination. Strategies for visual analysis have a long history and are widely accepted and easy to use. However, options for further quantification of intervention effects are becoming more widespread and expected. Using one or more of these summarization and analysis methods is important to ensure that the most accurate and appropriate decisions can be made.

References

Achenbach, T. M., & Edelbrock, C. S. (1978). The classification of child psychopathology: A review and analysis of empirical efforts. *Psychological Bulletin, 85,* 1275–1301.

Alberto, P. A., & Troutman, A. C. (2006). *Applied behavior analysis for teachers* (7th ed.). Upper Saddle River, NJ: Prentice Hall.

American Psychiatric Association. (2000). *Diagnostic and Statistical Manual of Mental Disorders* (4th ed., text rev.). Washington, DC: Author.

Angello, L. M., Volpe, R. J., Gureasko-Moore, S. P., Gureasko-Moore, D. P., Nebrig, M. R., Ota, K., et al. (2003). Assessment of attention deficit hyperactivity disorder: An evaluation of six published rating scales. *School Psychology Review, 32,* 241–262.

Ardoin, S. P., & Martens, B. K. (2004). Training children to make accurate self-evaluations: Effects on behavior and the quality of self-ratings. *Journal of Behavioral Education, 13,* 1–23.

Bloom, H., Hill, C., Black, A. R., & Lipsey, M. (2006, June). *Effect sizes in educational research: What they are, what they mean, and why they're important.* Presentation at the Institute for Education Sciences Conference, Washington, DC.

Bowditch, C. (1993). Getting rid of troublemakers: High school disciplinary procedures and the production of dropouts. *Social Problems, 40,* 493–507.

Bramlett, R. K. (1993). *The preschool observation code.* Unpublished manuscript, University of Central Arkansas, Conway.

Brown, T. E. (2001). *Brown Attention-Deficit Disorder Scales.* San Antonio, TX: Harcourt Assessment.

Busk, P. L., & Serlin, R. C. (1992). Meta-analysis for single-case research. In T. Kratochwill & J. R. Levin (Eds.), *Single-case research design and analysis* (pp. 187–212). Hillsdale, NJ: Erlbaum.

Chafouleas, S. M., Christ, T. J., Riley-Tillman, T. C., Briesch, A. M., & Chanese, J. A. (2007). Generalizability and dependability of Direct Behavior Ratings (DBRs) to assess social ehavior of preschoolers. *School Psychology Review.*

Chafouleas, S. M., McDougal, J. L., Riley-Tillman, T. C., Panahon, C. J., & Hilt, A. M. (2005). What do Daily Behavior Report Cards (DBRCs) measure? An initial comparison of DBRCs with direct observation for off-task behavior. *Psychology in the Schools, 42,* 669–676.

Chafouleas, S. M., Riley-Tillman, T. C., & McDougal, J. (2002). Good, bad, or in-between: How does the daily behavior report card rate? *Psychology in the Schools, 39,* 157–169.

Chafouleas, S. M., Riley-Tillman, T. C., & Sassu, K. A. (2006). Acceptability and reported use of Daily Behavior Report Cards among teachers. *Journal of Positive Behavior Interventions, 8,* 174–182.

Chafouleas, S. M., Riley-Tillman, T. C., Sassu, K. A., LaFrance, M. J., & Patwa, S. S. (2007). Daily behavior report cards (DBRCs): An investigation of consistency of on-task data across raters and method. *Journal of Positive Behavior Interventions, 9,* 30–37.

Cohen, J. (1988). *Statistical power analysis for the behavioral sciences* (2nd ed.). Hillsdale, NJ: Earlbaum.

Colvin, G., Kame'enui, E. J., & Sugai, G. (1993). School-wide and classroom management: Reconceptualizing the integration and management of students with behavior problems in general education. *Education and Treatment of Children, 16,* 361–381.

Cone, J. D. (1977). The relevance of reliability and validity for behavioral assessment. *Behavior Therapy, 8,* 411–426.

Cone, J. D. (1978). The behavioral assessment grid (BAG): A conceptual framework and a taxonomy. *Behavior Therapy, 9,* 882–888.

Crone, D. A., & Horner, R. H. (2003). *Building positive behavior support systems in schools: Functional behavioral assessment.* New York: Guilford Press.

Crone, D. A., Horner, R. H., & Hawken, L. S. (2004). *Responding to problem behavior in schools: The Behavior Education Program.* New York: Guilford Press.

Dalton, T. D., Martella, R. C., & Marchand-Martella, N. E. (1999). The effects of a self-management program in reducing off-task behavior. *Journal of Behavioral Education, 9,* 157–176.

Daly, E. J., Chafouleas, S., & Skinner, C. H. (2005). *Interventions for reading problems: Designing and evaluating effective strategies.* New York: The Guilford Press.

Dougherty, E. H., & Dougherty, A. (1977). The daily report card: A simplified and flexible package for classroom behavior management. In L. A. Hersov & M. Berger (Eds.), *Aggression and antisocial behavior in childhood and adolescence* pp. 73–93). London: Pergamon Press.

Dreger, R. M., Lewis, P. M., Rich, T. A., Miller, K. S., Reid, M. P., Overlade, D. C., et al. (1964). Behavioral classification project. *Journal of Consulting Psychology, 28,* 1–13.

Dumont, R., & Chafouleas, S. M. (1999). Conducting behavior observations: Some technical support? *Communiqué, 27*(7), 32–33.

Dunlap, G., Clarke, S., Jackson, M., Wright, S., Ramos, E., & Brinson, J. (1995). Self monitoring of classroom behaviors with students exhibiting emotional and behavioral challenges. *School Psychology Quarterly, 10,* 165–177.

DuPaul, G. J., Power, T. J., Anastopoulos, A. D., & Reid, R. (1998). *ADHD Rating Scale–IV.* New York: Guilford Press.

DuPaul, G. J., Power, T. J., Anastopoulos, A. D., Reid, R., McGoey, K., & Ikeda, M. (1997). Teacher ratings of attention-deficit/hyperactivity disorder: Factor structure and normative data. *Psychological Assessment, 9,* 436–444.

Dwyer, K. P., Osher, D., & Hoffman, C. C. (2000). Creating responsive schools: Contextualizing early warning, timely response. *Exceptional Children, 66,* 347–365.

Erchul, W. P., & Martens, B. K. (2002). *School consultation: Conceptual and empirical bases of practice* (2nd ed.). New York: Plenum Press.

Ervin, R. A., Schaughnency, E., Matthews, A., Goodman, S. D., & McGlinchey, M. T. (2007). Primary and secondary prevention of behavior difficulties: Developing a data-informed problem-solving model to guide decision making at a schoolwide level. *Psychology in the Schools, 44,* 7–18.

Gadow, K. D., Sprafkin, J., & Nolan, E. E. (1996). *ADHD School Observation Code.* Stony Brook, NY: Checkmate Plus.

Glenn, H. (2001). A review of the BASC Monitor for ADHD. In B. S. Plake & J. C. Impara (Eds.), *The fourteenth mental measurements yearbook* (pp. 109–110). Lincoln: University of Nebraska Press.

Good, R. H., III, Simmons, D. C., & Kame'enui, E. J. (2001). The importance of decision-making utility of a continuum of fluency-based indicators of foundational reading skills for third-grade high-stakes outcomes. *Scientific Studies of Reading, 5,* 257–288.

Gottfredson, D. C., Gottfredson, G. D., & Hybl, L. G. (1993). Managing adolescent behavior: A multiyear, multischool study. *American Educational Research Journal, 30,* 179–215.

Greenwood, C. R., Carta, J. J., Kamps, D., Terry, B., & Delquadri, J. (1994). Development and validation of standard classroom observation systems for school practitioners: Ecobehavioral assessment systems software (EBASS). *Exceptional Children, 61,* 197–210.

Hey, L., Nelson, R., & Hay, W. (1977). Some methodological problems in the use of teachers as observers. *Journal of Applied Behavior Analysis, 10,* 345–348.

Hey, L., Nelson, R., & Hay, W. (1980). Methodological problems in the use of participant observers. *Journal of Applied Behavior Analysis, 13,* 501–504.

Hintze, J. M., & Matthews, W. J. (2004). The generalizability of systematic direct observations across time and setting: A preliminary investigation of the psychometrics of behavioral observations. *School Psychology Review, 33,* 258–270.

Hintze, J. M., Christ, T. J., & Methe, S. A. (2006). Curriculum-based assessment. *Psychology in the Schools, 43*, 45–56.

Hintze, J. M., Volpe, R. J., & Shapiro, E. S. (2002). Best practices in the systematic direct observation of student behavior. In A. Thomas & J. Grimes (Eds.), *Best practices in school psychology* (4th ed., pp. 993–1006). Bethesda, MD: National Association of School Psychologists.

Horner, R. H., & Sugai, G. (2001). "Data" need not be a four-letter word: Using data to improve schoolwide discipline. *Beyond Behavior, 11*, 20–22.

Horner, R. H., Todd, A. W., & Lewis Palmer, T. (2005). Schoolwide positive behavior support. L. M. Bambara & L. Kern (Eds.), *Individualized supports for students with problem behaviors: Designing positive behavior plans* (pp. 359–390). New York: Guilford Press.

Hosp, M. K., Hosp, J. L., & Howell, K. W. (2007). *The ABCs of CBM: A practical guide to curriculum-based measurement*. New York: Guilford Press.

Howell, K. W., & Nolet, V. (2000). *Curriculum-based evaluation: Teaching and decision making* (3rd ed.). Belmont, CA: Wadsworth.

Howell, K. W., Zucker, S. H., & Moorehead, M. K. (2000). *Multilevel Academic Skills Inventory*. Bellingham, WA: Western Washington University, Applied Research and Development Center.

Hyman, I. A., & Perone, D. C. (1998). The other side of school violence: Educator policies and practices that may contribute to student misbehavior. *Journal of School Psychology, 36*, 7–27.

Irvin, L. K., Horner, R. H., Ingram, K., Todd, A. W., Sugai, G., Sampson, N. K., et al. (2006). Using discipline referral data for decision making about student behavior in elementary and middle schools: An empirical evaluation of validity. *Journal of Positive Behavior Interventions, 8*, 10–23.

Irvin, L. K., Tobin, T. J., Sprague, J. R., Sugai, G., & Vincent, C. G. (2004). Validity of discipline referral measures as indices of school-wide behavioral status and effects of school-wide behavioral interventions. *Journal of Positive Behavior Interventions, 6*, 3–12.

Jenkins, J. (2003) A review of the ADHD Rating Scale–IV. In B. S. Plake, J. C. Impara, & R. A. Spies (Eds.), *The fifteenth mental measurements yearbook* (pp. 19–23). Lincoln, NE: University of Nebraska Press.

Jenkins, J. R., Deno, S. L., & Mirkin, P. K. (1979). Measuring pupil progress toward the least restrictive alternative. *Learning Disability Quarterly, 2*, 81–91.

Jenson, W. R., Rhode, G., & Reavis, H. K. (1994). *The tough kid tool box*. Longmont, CO: Sopris West.

Jones, K. (2001). A review of the BASC Monitor for ADHD. In B. S. Plake & J. C. Impara (Eds.), *The fourteenth mental measurements yearbook* (pp. 110–112). Lincoln, NE: University of Nebraska Press.

Kazdin, A. E. (1982). *Single-case research designs: Methods for clinical and applied settings*. New York: Oxford University Press.

Kehle, T. J., Clark, E., & Jenson, W. R. (1986). Effectiveness of self-observation with disordered elementary school children. *School Psychology Review, 15*, 289–295.

Kratochwill, T. R., Sheridan, S. M., Carlson, J. S., & Lasecki, K. L. (1999). Advances in behavioral assessment. In C. Reynolds & T. Gutkin (Eds.), *The handbook of school psychology* (3rd ed., pp. 350–382). New York: Wiley.

Lane, K. L., O'Shaughnessy, T. E., Lambros, K. M., Gresham, F. M., & Beebe-Frankenberger, M. E. (2002). The efficacy of phonological awareness training with first-grade students who have behavior problems. *Journal of Emotional and Behavioral Disorders, 9*, 219–231.

Leff, S. S., & Lakin, R. (2005). Playground-based observational systems: A review and implications for practitioners and researchers. *School Psychology Review, 34*, 475–489.

Lewis, T. J., & Sugai, G. (1999). Effective behavior support: A systems approach to proactive school-wide management. *Focus on Exceptional Children, 31*, 1–24.

Lindskog, C. (2003). A review of the ADHD Rating Scale–IV. In B. S. Plake, J. C. Impara, & R. A. Spies (Eds.), *The fifteenth mental measurements yearbook* (pp. 23–25). Lincoln, NE: University of Nebraska Press.

Lipsey, M. W. (1990). *Design sensitivity: Statistical power for experimental research*. Newbury Park, CA: Sage.

Maag, J. W., Rutherford, R. B., & DiGangi, S. A. (1992). Effects of self-monitoring and contingent reinforcement on on-task behavior and academic productivity of learning-disabled students: A social validation study. *Psychology in the Schools, 29*, 157–172.

Martin, S. (2001). *!Observe: A behavior recording and reporting software program* (2nd ed.). Longmont, CO: Sopris West.

Mash, E. J., & Wolfe, D. A. (1999). *Abnormal child psychology*. Belmont, CA: Wadsworth.

Mayer, M. J., & Leone, P. E. (1999). A structural analysis of school violence and disruption: Implications for creating safer schools. *Education and Treatment of Children, 22,* 333–358.

McCurdy, B. L., Mannella, M. C., & Eldridge, N. (2003). Positive behavior support in urban schools: Can we prevent the escalation of antisocial behavior? *Journal of Positive Behavioral Interventions, 5,* 158–170.

McDougal, J., Chafouleas, S. M., & Waterman, B. (2006). *A practitioner's guide to functional assessment and behavior intervention in schools.* Champaign, IL: Research Press.

McEvoy, A., & Welker, R. (2000). Antisocial behavior, academic failure, and school climate: A critical review. *Journal of Emotional and Behavioral Disorders, 8,* 130–141.

McFadden, A. C., Marsh, G. E., Price, B. J., & Hwang, Y. (1992). A study of race and gender bias in the punishment of school children. *Education and Treatment of Children, 15,* 140–146.

Merrell, K. W. (2000). Informant reports: Theory and research in using child behavior rating scales in school settings. In E. S. Shapiro & T. R. Kratochwill (Eds.), *Behavioral assessment in schools: Theory, research, and clinical foundations* (pp. 233–256). New York: Guilford Press.

Merrell, K. W. (2003). *Behavioral, social, and emotional assessment of children and adolescents* (2nd ed.). Mahwah, NJ: Erlbaum.

Merrell, K. W., Ervin, R. A., & Gimpel, G. A. (2006). *School psychology for the 21st century: Foundations and practices.* New York: Guilford Press.

Metzler, C. W., Biglan, A., Rusby, J. C., & Sprague, J. R. (2001). Evaluation of a comprehensive behavior management program to improve school-wide positive behavior support. *Education and Treatment of Children, 24,* 448–479.

Morrison, G. M., & D'Incau, B. (2000). Developmental and service trajectories of students with disabilities recommended for expulsion from school. *Exceptional Children, 66,* 257–272.

Morrison, G. M., & Skiba, R. (2001). Predicting violence from school misbehavior: Promises and perils. *Psychology in the Schools, 38,* 173–184.

National Association of School Psychologists. (2000). *Standards for training and field placement programs in school psychology.* Bethesda, MD: Author.

Nelson, J. R., Benner, G. J., Reid, R., Epstein, M. H., & Currin, D. (2002). An investigation of the convergent validity of office referrals with the Child Behavior Checklist Teacher Report Form. *Journal of Emotional and Behavioral Disorders, 10,* 181–189.

Noell, G. H., Duhon, G. J., Gatti, S. L., & Connell, J. E. (2002). Consultation, follow-up, and implementation of behavior management interventions in general education. *School Psychology Review, 31,* 217–234.

Oswald, L. K. (2000). *Comprehensive Behavior Tracking System* [computer software]. Salt Lake City, UT: Designer Edge Software.

Piersel, W. C. (1985). Self-observation and completion of school assignments: The influence of a physical recording device and expectancy characteristics. *Psychology in the Schools, 22,* 331–336.

Ramsay, M. C., Reynolds, C. R., & Kamphaus, R. W. (2002). *Essentials of behavioral assessment.* New York: Wiley.

Reinke, W. M., & Herman, K. C. (2002). Creating school environments that deter antisocial behaviors in youth. *Psychology in the Schools, 39,* 549–559.

Reynolds, C. R., & Kamphaus, R. W. (2004a). *Behavior Assessment System for Children* (2nd ed.). Bloomington, MN: Pearson Assessments.

Reynolds, C. R., & Kamphaus, R. W. (2004b). *Student Observation System.* Circle Pines, MN: AGS Publishing.

Reynolds, C. R., & Kamphaus, R. W. (2006). *BASC-2 Portable Observation System.* Circle Pines, MN: AGS Publishing.

Richards, S. B., Taylor, R., Ramasamy, R., & Richards, R. Y. (1999). *Single-subject research: Application in educational and clinical settings.* Belmont, CA: Wadsworth.

Riley-Tillman, T. C., & Chafouleas, S. M. (2003). Using interventions that exist in the natural environment to increase treatment integrity and social influence. *Journal of Educational and Psychological Consultation, 14,* 139–156.

Riley-Tillman, T. C., Chafouleas, S. M., Briesch, A. M., & Eckert, T. E. (2007). *The decision reliability and acceptability of Daily Behavior Report Cards.* Unpublished manuscript.

Riley-Tillman, T. C., Chafouleas, S. M., Sassu, K. A., Chanese, J. A., & Glazer, A. D. (in press). Examining agreement between Direct Behavior Ratings (DBRs) and systematic direct observation data for on-task and disruptive behavior. *Journal of Positive Behavior Interventions.*

Riley-Tillman, T. C., Kalberer, S. M., & Chafouleas, S. M. (2005). Selecting the right tool for the job: A review of behavior monitoring tools used to assess student response to intervention. *California School Psychologist, 10*, 81–92.

Rock, M. L. (2005). Use of strategic self-monitoring to enhance academic engagement, productivity, and accuracy of students with and without exceptionalities. *Journal of Positive Behavior Interventions, 7*, 3–17.

Rose, T. L. (1988). Current disciplinary practices with handicapped students: Suspensions and expulsions. *Exceptional Children, 55*, 230–239.

Safran, S. P., & Oswald, K. (2003). Positive behavior supports: Can schools reshape disciplinary practices? *Exceptional Children, 69*, 361–373.

Salvia, J., & Ysseldyke, J. E. (2004). *Assessment* (9th ed.). Princeton, NJ: Houghton Mifflin.

Sandoval, J., & Echandia, A. (1994). Behavior Assessment System for Children. *Journal of School Psychology, 32*, 419–425.

Sattler, J. M. (2002). *Assessment of children: Behavioral and clinical applications* (4th ed.). San Diego: Author.

Saudargas, R. A. (1997). *State–Event Classroom Observation System (SECOS)*. Unpublished manuscript, University of Tennessee–Knoxville.

Saudargas, R. A., & Lentz, F. E. (1986). Estimating percent of time and rate via direct observation: A suggested observational procedure and format. *School Psychology Review, 15*, 36–48.

Schwartz, I. S., & Baer, D. M. (1991). Social validity assessments: Is current practice state of the art? *Journal of Applied Behavior Analysis, 24*, 189–204.

Scott, T. M. (2001). A schoolwide example of positive behavioral support. *Journal of Positive Behavior Interventions, 3*, 88–94.

Scott, T. M., & Barrett, S. B. (2004). Using staff and student time engaged in disciplinary procedures to evaluate the impact of school-wide PBS. *Journal of Positive Behavior Interventions, 6*, 21–28.

Shapiro, E. S. (1996). *Academic skills problems workbook*. New York: Guilford Press.

Shapiro, E. S. (2004). *Academic skills problems workbook* (rev. ed.). New York: Guilford Press.

Shapiro, E. S., & Cole, C. L. (1994). *Behavior change in the classroom: Self-management interventions*. New York: Guilford Press.

Shapiro, E. S., & Kratochwill, T. R. (Eds.). (2000). *Behavioral assessment in schools* (2nd ed.). New York: Guilford Press.

Shinn, M. R. (Ed.). (1989). *Curriculum-based measurement: Assessing special children*. New York: Guilford Press.

Shinn, M. R. (Ed.). (1998). *Advanced applications of curriculum-based measurement*. New York: Guilford Press.

Skiba, R. J., & Peterson, R. L. (1999). The dark side of zero tolerance: Can punishment lead to safe schools? *Phi Delta Kappan, 80*, 372–382.

Skiba, R. J., & Peterson, R. L. (2000). School discipline at a crossroads: From zero tolerance to early response. *Exceptional Children, 66*, 335–347.

Skiba, R. J., Peterson, R. L., & Williams, T. (1997). Office referrals and suspension: Disciplinary intervention in middle schools. *Education and Treatment of Children, 20*, 1–21.

Smith, D. J., Young, K. R., West, R. P., Morgan, D. P., & Rhode, G. (1988). Reducing the disruptive behavior of junior high school students: A classroom self-management procedure. *Behavioral Disorders, 13*, 231–239.

Sparrow, S. S., Cicchetti, D. V., & Balla, D. A. (2005). *Vineland Adaptive Behavior Scales* (2nd ed.). Circle Pines, MN: American Guidance Service.

Sprague, J. R., Sugai, G., Horner, R. H., & Walker, H. M. (1999). Using discipline referral data to evaluate school-wide discipline and violence prevention interventions. *Oregon School Studies Council Bulletin, 42*, 1–17.

Steege, M. W., Davin, T., & Hathaway, M. (2001). Reliability and accuracy of a performance-based behavioral recording procedure. *School Psychology Review, 30*, 252–261.

Sugai, G., & Horner, R. H. (2002). The evolution of discipline practices: School-wide positive behavior supports. *Child and Family Behavior Therapy, 24*, 23–50.

Sugai, G., Horner, R. H., Dunlap, G., Hieneman, M., Lewis, T. J., Nelson, C. M., et al. (2000). Applying positive behavioral support and functional behavioral assessment in schools. *Journal of Positive Behavior Interventions, 2*, 131–143.

Sugai, G., Sprague, J. R., Horner, R. H., & Walker, H. M. (2000). Preventing school violence: The use of discipline referrals to assess and monitor school-wide discipline interventions. *Journal of Emotional and Behavioral Disorders, 8,* 94–101.

Taylor-Greene, S., Brown, D., Nelson, L., Longton, J., Gassman, T., Cohen, J., et al. (1997). School-wide behavioral support: Starting the year off right. *Journal of Behavioral Education, 7,* 99–112.

Thompson, B. (2006). *Foundations of behavioral statistics: An insight-based approach.* New York: Guilford Press.

Tobin, T., & Sugai, G. (1999a). Predicting violence at school, chronic discipline problems, and high school outcomes from sixth graders' school records. *Journal of Emotional and Behavioral Disorders, 7,* 40–53.

Tobin, T., & Sugai, G. (1999b). Discipline problems, placements, and outcomes for students with serious emotional disturbance. *Behavioral Disorders, 24,* 109–121.

Tobin, T., Sugai, G., & Colvin, G. (1996). Patterns in middle school discipline records. *Journal of Emotional and Behavioral Disorders, 4,* 82–94.

Tobin, T., Sugai, G., & Colvin, G. (May, 2000). Research brief: Using discipline referrals to make decisions. *Bulletin of the National Association of Secondary Principals, 84,* 106–120.

Todd, A. W., Horner, R. H., & Sugai, G. (1999). Self-monitoring and self-recruited praise: Effects on problem behavior, academic engagement, and work completion in a typical classroom. *Journal of Positive Behavior Interventions, 1,* 66–76.

Torgesen, J. K., Wagner, R. K., Rashotte, C. A., Rose, E., Lindamood, P., Conway, T., et al. (1999). Preventing reading failure in young children with phonological processing disabilities: Group and individual responses to instruction. *Journal of Educational Psychology, 91,* 579–593.

Townsend, B. L. (2000). The disproportionate discipline of African American learners: Reducing school suspensions and expulsions. *Exceptional Children, 66,* 381–391.

Trzesniewski, K. H., Moffitt, T. E., Caspi, A., Taylor, A., & Maughan, B. (2006). Revisiting the association between reading achievement and antisocial behavior: New evidence of an environmental explanation from a twin study. *Child Development, 77,* 72–88.

Walker, H. M., Horner, R. H., Sugai, G., Bullis, M., Sprague, J. R., Bricker, D., et al. (1996). Integrated approaches to preventing antisocial behavior patterns among school-age children and youth. *Journal of Emotional and Behavioral Disorders, 4,* 193–256.

Walker, H. M., & Severson, H. H. (1991). *Systematic screening for behavior disorders.* Longmont, CO: Sopris West.

Watkins, M. W. (1998). *MacKappa* [computer software]. University Park, PA: Author.

Watkins, M. W., & Pacheco, M. (2000). Interobserver agreement in behavioral research: Importance and calculation. *Journal of Behavioral Education, 10,* 205–212.

White, R., Algozzine, B., Audette, R., Marr, M. B., & Ellis, E. D., Jr. (2001). Unified discipline: A school-wide approach for managing problem behavior. *Intervention in School and Clinic, 37,* 3–8.

Wolery, M., Bailey, D. B., & Sugai, G. M. (1988). *Effective teaching: Principles and procedures of applied behavior analysis with exceptional students.* Boston: Allyn & Bacon.

Wolf, M. M. (1978). Social validity: The case for subjective measurement or how applied behavior analysis is finding its heart. *Journal of Applied Behavior Analysis, 11,* 203–214.

Wood, S. J., Murdock, J. Y., Cronin, M. E., Dawson, N. M., & Kirby, P. C. (1998). Effects of self monitoring on on-task behaviors of at-risk middle school students. *Journal of Behavioral Education, 8,* 263–279.

Worthen, B. R., Borg, W. R., & White, K. R. (1993). *Measurement and evaluation in the schools: A practical guide.* White Plains, NY: Longman.

Wright, J. (2002). Behavior Report Card Generator [computer software]. Retrieved November 15, 2005, from *www. jimwrightonline.com/php/tbrc/tbrc.php*

Wright, J. A., & Dusek, J. B. (1998). Compiling school base rates for disruptive behaviors from student disciplinary referral data. *School Psychology Review, 27,* 138–147.

Index